Teaching Gifted Children 4–7

A Guide for Teachers

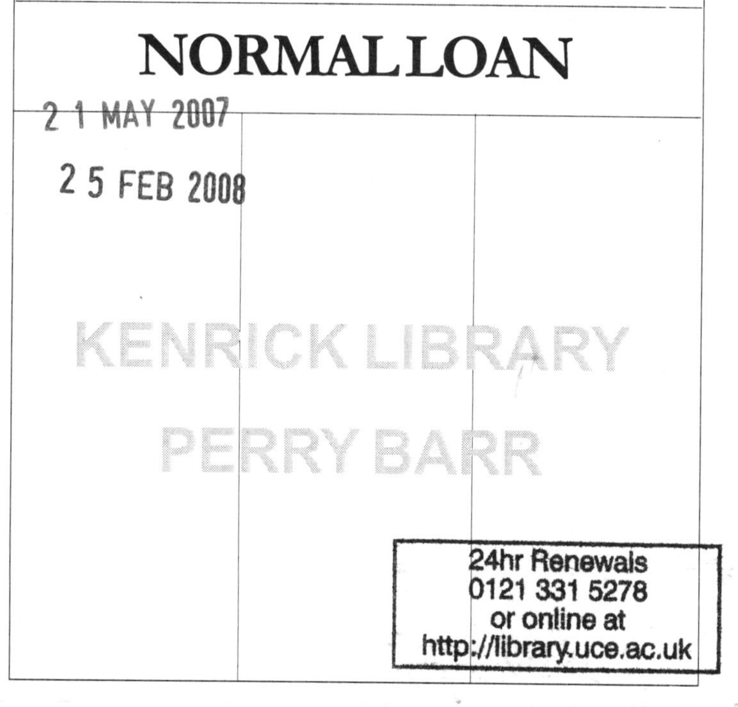

David Fulton Publishers
London

I dedicate this book to the memory of my Father. I regret that he has not lived to see me strive for self-fulfilment by reaching out to help young children to do the same.

David Fulton Publishers Ltd
The Chiswick Centre, 414 Chiswick High Road, London W4 5TF

www.fultonpublishers.co.uk

First published in Great Britain by David Fulton Publishers 2002

British Library Cataloguing in Publication Data
A catalogue record for this book is available from the British Library.

ISBN 1–85346–877–0

Contents

Acknowledgements

Over the past seven years, many people have helped me to develop my interest and research about gifted and talented children. Exploring aspects of provision for younger children has been both exciting and challenging for me. Meeting and working with children aged 4–7 has given me hours of joy, but at the same time it made me realise the complexity of addressing issues of giftedness in younger children. It is not possible to name all those who have helped me to write this book, but I would like to thank the following organisations and people:

- Teachers from Richmond, Hounslow and Wandsworth LEAs, who contributed ideas during in-service sessions.
- Yvonne Perret, for carrying out a small-scale research study in Cambridgeshire LEA, which highlighted useful examples of good practice.
- Gill Rose for trialling activities with young children in two Wandsworth schools, Highview Primary School and Honeywell Infants School.
- Nelson-Thornes Publishers for giving permision to reproduce artwork in Figures 5.9–5.16.

Introduction

The first years of schooling are a time for changes: from home to school, moving on to a springboard of wider learning which can create feelings of excitement, contentment or frustration. Much of what happens depends on the teacher and the other adults who work with the children. The first years can be a sea of change offering anything from boredom in still, shallow waters to excitement on wave after wave of exploration into areas of new ideas. The spectrum from boredom to excitement during this time needs the navigating skills of a sensitive, well-informed teacher who can guide the young child through an appropriate course for several hours each day. A gifted child, no matter how the word 'gifted' is defined, has the potential to provide much to others in future years. This will happen if that child is guided and nurtured with a significant degree of informed and pragmatic wisdom in the first years of his or her school life.

Teachers and classroom assistants who work in nursery or infant classrooms have a range of professional skills and a high degree of empathy and understanding. This book is designed to offer them guidance to steer gifted children towards self-fulfilment. It is essentially a practical guide which takes into account the realities of classroom situations. Theoretical components, drawn from a range of authoritative sources, provide a sound background for the content of this book. These are kept brief, but readers should be able to pursue matters of interest by using the references provided.

The book is written in an interactive style. Readers are invited to contribute their own ideas and reflect on what is presented. To the extent that the book contributes to forging educationally sound partnerships between the gifted child, teachers and parents the writing of it will have been justified.

The book is divided into seven chapters. Chapter 1 sets out the context of the book and provides a general background on the topic of gifted young children. The importance of provision in the first years of schooling is emphasised. Recent national developments on the education of gifted children are discussed. With the help of five case studies of children, a number of issues are raised and the complexity of identifying younger gifted children is highlighted.

Chapter 2 focuses on aspects of identification. Different perspectives on the nature of giftedness are considered. Drawing on theory and research, an effort is made to provide the reader with a conceptual map of the various viewpoints on giftedness. Howard Gardner's theory of multiple intelligences, which is used as a framework for both identification and provision, is introduced in this chapter. Strategies for identification from multiple sources are discussed. The important role of parents in the identification process is highlighted. A number of checklists of cognitive and affective attributes of gifted children are introduced.

Effective provision for able children does not happen by accident: it evolves from the concerted efforts of all those who are involved in educating them. An analysis of the cognitive needs of gifted children is undertaken before discussing strategies for enhancing classroom provision. The importance of providing a rich classroom environment is stressed. The role of questions in extending children's thinking is discussed. A framework for curriculum differentiation, based on Bloom's Taxonomy, is introduced in this chapter. How young children's curiosity and imagination can be channelled into creative productivity is explored. A wealth of examples is used to make the various principles accessible to the reader.

The focus of Chapter 4 is the individual needs of the gifted child and how we can organise learning by taking these into account. The process of *Curriculum Compacting* and the appropriate use of the time released by streamlining what the child already knows are discussed. The importance of encouraging children to develop their passion for topics and taking note of their individual learning styles are brought to the readers' attention. The role of teacher assessment and the positive impact of children developing individual portfolios are considered in this chapter. The role of adults in supporting the gifted child is explored. This chapter also considers aspects of organisation, such as early entry and the continuing debate on acceleration and enrichment as strategies to extend gifted children.

Aspects of subject-specific provision are discussed in Chapter 5. Extending children's learning through mathematics, English and ICT is the main thrust of this chapter. Attributes of young, promising mathematicians and the gifted language learner are considered and, based on these attributes, strategies for extending learning opportunities are discussed. The potential of ICT, especially the computer with its power and speed, is explored, and a number of examples of the practical classroom use of ICT are given.

Chapter 6 is devoted to a consideration of the social and emotional needs of gifted children. The recent shift in thinking with regard to provision for gifted children – from a purely cognitive point of view to including affective aspects – is highlighted. Gifted children, by virtue of being faster learners, may face some unusual challenges. These are considered, and a number of strategies to meet these particular challenges, are suggested.

Finally, Chapter 7 looks at the selection and use of resources to support high quality learning for gifted young children. Desirable attributes of a teacher of the young gifted child are considered. An audit for assessing the quality of provision for gifted children and guidance on drawing up a school policy are given. This chapter also provides a list of resources and details of organisations which support the special needs of gifted children.

1 The young gifted child: setting the context

General background

Recognising and nurturing young children's abilities and interests is an exciting challenge. It is exciting because younger children are often hungry for knowledge; they are curious and are more forthcoming with imaginative ideas. They have unique personalities and specific abilities which need to be identified so that we can do everything in our power to help these young people to make the most of their special strengths and realise their full potential. They may show all-round ability or demonstrate special strengths or aptitudes in academic areas such as English, mathematics and science. Some may, in addition, demonstrate special behavioural characteristics such as organisational ability and leadership skills from a very young age. The challenge for the teacher is not only to recognise the multiple talents of the child, but also to think of ways of acknowledging these talents and, of course, to then apply the most effective strategies to nurture all their talents. By doing so, we are more likely to support young children to develop their self-esteem and confidence. They will also be encouraged to take pleasure in learning, thereby contributing to their development into well-rounded personalities.

I have always wondered whether we feel an extra sense of responsibility to do our best for younger children because they are more vulnerable and perhaps more dependent on adults than older children. Without proper support younger children's curiosity could be stifled, their 'play and exploration' time could be curtailed for what they may feel is considered more 'serious' and 'proper' work, and they may feel that using their imagination is unimportant and not worthwhile. Yet curiosity, play and imagination are the essence of a creative mind which is what we are always striving to encourage.

The issues I have raised are by no means limited to the education of younger children. Why are they particularly important when considering able younger children? First, habits are formed very early in life. Attitudes and styles of learning as well as self-perceptions developed during the first years of schooling will most certainly influence future learning. In addition, gaps in their knowledge and understanding could lead to disinterest in school and lower achievement.

Research evidence tells us that external stimulation can enhance learning potential of children in the early years of their lives. Studies (Vaughn. *et al.* 1991; Fowler *et al.*

1995, quoted in Porter 1999) suggest that provision of enrichment activities and early interventions help to raise achievement levels of younger children significantly. As children are receptive to new ideas and cognitive restructuring at a greater speed in the first few years of their lives, time and effort given to them will be worthwhile. This is applicable to all children, but is particularly important in the case of children who may not, for all sorts of reasons, receive the stimulation they need in their homes. I will discuss the issue of the importance of early identification and enrichment further in Chapter 2.

There is an ongoing debate among educators of young children whether children should be labelled 'gifted' before they are seven or eight years old. This debate does not pose a problem for the approach I have adopted for writing this book because the model I am using is based on a two-way process, as shown below, when dealing with children who show high ability in one or more areas.

Provision ⇄ **Identification of ability**

Whatever terminology we use to describe children who demonstrate higher ability, what matters most is what we provide for them in the classroom. For example, in the two-way process of 'provision and identification' the emphasis is on maximising 'opportunities' for children so that they will show their potential talents. Observation and identification of special strengths, 'gifts' or 'talents' will then enable teachers to make appropriate provision based on their observations.

My reference to 'gifted' children refers to observed and recorded special abilities which should help adults to build up profiles of the children. If a list of academically 'gifted' children's names is required at any stage, the profile should assist in composing that list.

The national scene on educating the gifted and talented

In England and Wales, the past few years have witnessed the introduction of several initiatives by the government to support the education of the gifted and talented. There has also been a number of significant developments in aspects relating to general (not specifically relating to gifted children) provision for children in the early years. At the time of writing this book, discussions on introducing new extension tests – introducing a level 3* in academic subjects at the end of Key Stage 1 – are taking place. The purpose of these tests is to assess children's in-depth knowledge in subjects so that these can be acknowledged earlier in their school life.

Before we consider national developments on gifted education, it will be useful for you to reflect for a moment and write down how you would define giftedness. During in-service sessions I often ask teachers to put their hands up if they thought they were 'gifted'. Only one or two out of about forty participants ever put their hands up. When we discuss why they did not feel they were 'gifted', the reason which often emerges is that they have difficulty interpreting what I mean by being 'gifted'. *'Do you mean exceptionally good at everything or at some things?'* is one question they often ask. It is interesting to note that many more teachers say that they are particularly 'good at some things, but not at everything' and if that definition was used, many more would feel they were 'gifted'. As discussed elsewhere (Koshy and Casey 1997a), based on over 600 teachers' evaluations of the effectiveness of our in-service courses on gifted education, teachers find the discussions of various terminology used to refer to higher ability children to be one of the most useful aspects of the course. What usually emerges after the discussions is that we *really are* referring to children who show higher ability in all or some areas of the curriculum. This working definition is useful for what we do in our classrooms.

According to the DfES definition, the term 'gifted' refers to those with high ability or potential in academic subjects, and 'talented' refers to those with high ability or potential in the expressive or creative arts or sport. This is the terminology which is also used for OFSTED inspections.

Concerns about the lack of provision for gifted children have been voiced by many for at least three decades. Her Majesty's Inspectorate asserted (HMI 1992) that the needs of the very able were not being met in many schools and that such pupils were not sufficiently challenged. Around the same time Alexander *et al.*(1992) pointed out that there was 'obsessive fear' in some schools about being deemed 'elitist' and as a consequence 'the needs of some of our most able have quite simply not been met'. And – for those who felt uneasy about focusing on the needs of the able – HMI Mackintosh (Ofsted 1994, p. 13) had this to say:

> There is very clear evidence that focusing sharply on what the most able can achieve raises the expectations generally, because essentially it involves consideration of the organisation and management of teaching and learning.

Many Ofsted inspection reports also highlighted the need for providing more intellectual challenge in classroom activities. So what is on offer for the gifted and talented?

In 1997 (DfEE) the government announced in the White Paper entitled *Excellence in Schools*:

> We plan to develop a strategy for the early identification and support of particularly able and talented children. We want every school and local education authority to plan how it will help gifted and talented children.

An inquiry by the House of Commons Select Committee (1999) highlighted the problems many schools experience in offering an appropriate curriculum for the gifted, and declared that this aspect of education needed attention. The main areas of concern were the lack of high expectations from gifted children and the need for schools and teachers to have a better understanding of ways in which provision can be improved. As a result, in March 1999, the government launched the 'Excellence in Cities' (DfEE 1999) initiative for raising the achievement of pupils in inner-city areas. As part of this, all participating secondary and primary schools were required to:

- Identify their 5 to 10 per cent 'gifted and talented' pupils. The percentage refers to the schools' intake, not the whole school population. In practice, the most able within a school would be referred to as the 'gifted and talented' pupils.
- Appoint a coordinator responsible for the education of these pupils.
- Implement a distinct teaching and learning programme for the gifted and talented.

At the present time, funding is provided only for schools in local education authorities within the Excellence in Cities areas, but other forms of support have been offered to all schools. These include support publications, from the DfES, for teaching numeracy and literacy (DfES 2000a), and materials from the QCA, entitled 'Teaching Gifted and Talented Pupils in Mathematics and English at Key stage 1 and 2' (See Chapter 7 for resources). World-class tests are available for gifted and talented pupils in mathematics and problem-solving at the ages of 9 and 13 from QCA. These may be taken by children at an earlier age if they feel ready for them.

Two years after the start of a national drive for improving educational opportunities for gifted children, where are we now? One of the concerns highlighted in the research carried out at Brunel University (Thomas *et al.* 1996) looking at provision for gifted children, using a national sample, was teachers' lack of understanding of strategies for classroom provision. An evaluation of 'gifted and talented' provision carried out by Ofsted (2001) acknowledges that a promising start has been made. As the following points among the recommendations for improvement are particularly relevant to the context of this book, they are summarised below:

- Schools would benefit more generally from greater help on assessment and forms of teaching which support higher achievement at an earlier stage.
- The identification of gifted and talented pupils has presented difficulties for schools. To date, methods of identification have generally been rudimentary and have not yet solved the problem of recognising latent high ability, particularly among pupils who are underachieving generally.
- There is a need for greater engagement of parents and pupils.
- Schools need to establish a secure basis for improving mainstream teaching.

Two aspects emerge from what has been presented in the previous section: (1) schools need to think about effective procedures for the identification of gifted and talented children, and (2) they need to devise strategies for effective classroom provision. To help me to set up some expectations for writing this book, I carried out a survey of schools in six LEAs – three from the Excellence in Cities areas and three others – as a needs analysis exercise which formed part of the work of Brunel University's able children's education centre. The following useful points emerged from the survey.

- Many nursery and infant teachers felt they have not been provided with adequate internal or external support with aspects of identification or provision.
- Only three out of 12 infant teachers and none of the four nursery teachers in schools where there were school policies for 'gifted and talented' children said they knew the contents of those policies.

- Fourteen out of the 18 infant and nursery teachers who took part in the survey felt there was very little coverage of issues relating to provision for younger children at both short and longer in-service courses.
- There was a serious shortage of books and resources directly targeting issues relating to the education of younger gifted and talented children.

Although the size of the sample used in this survey was small it did highlight the need for writing this book. I also recollect what one DfES 'gifted and talented' officer, Richard Smith, pointed out to me, during a discussion I had with him prior to leading a seminar on improving provision for Key Stage 1 children, at the Gifted and Talented Standing Conference (March 2002): *'What we need to remember is that if there are gifted and talented pupils at Key Stages 2 to 4, then surely they were 'gifted' at Key Stage 1 and prior to that and we need to provide for them.'* I knew what he meant: they don't just jump into a gifted category from a mental vacuum.

My reason for writing this book is to support the identification and provision of gifted and talented children during the Nursery and Key Stage 1 phases of education. Focusing on children's special abilities, gifts or talents – whatever terminology we care to use to refer to them – has two clear benefits:

1. Recognition of talents enables teachers to make appropriate provision at a crucial time of children's development.
2. Gathering of evidence of children's strengths provides a rich bank of information when making judgements about children at a later stage.

It is my hope that reading this book will provide those who are involved in educating younger children with a clearer understanding of issues relating to giftedness and aspects of provision. As mentioned above, at present there is very little guidance available to support teachers. A review of the many excellent documents that have been produced to offer support to early years educationists in the last five years reveals that very little reference is made to matters relating to gifted and talented education. However, what many of these publications offer is guidance and a set of principles on good early years provision and can be drawn on to form a firm foundation when considering the identification of and provision for gifted and talented children. In the following section I will consider some of these principles which will permeate the contents of this book.

Early years provision

As the content of this book covers aspects of identification and provision for the age group 4–7, we need to give considerable attention to the Early Learning Goals set out by the QCA. Let us especially take note of the opening section:

> Early childhood is a crucial stage of life in terms of children's physical, intellectual, emotional and social development and their well being. Growth is both rapid and differential. A significant proportion of learning takes place from birth to age six.

> It is a time when children particularly need high quality care and learning experiences. (QCA 1999: 4)

Through initiatives such as Sure Start, Early Excellence Centres and enhanced provision in nursery and reception classes, the government is making significant efforts to improve provision for younger children. At present, baseline assessment takes place for all children at the beginning of their school life; this should provide some valuable information when judging children's particular strengths and their special learning needs.

Principles of early years provision

I have tried to take account of the principles set out by the QCA for early years provision in guiding me to incorporate them into the contents of this book. The following elements, summarised below, are particularly relevant in making effective provision for gifted and talented children:

- Effective education requires both a relevant curriculum and practitioners who understand and are able to implement the curriculum requirements.
- Early years experience should build on what children know and can do.
- To be effective, an early years curriculum needs to be carefully structured. In that structure there should be three strands: provision for the different points from which children are starting, building on what they do and matching what is taught to the child's appropriate level.
- A well-planned and well-organised learning environment that gives children rich and stimulating experience.

Thinking about gifted and talented children – making a start

Think of a child in your class, or a child you have recently taught, who you would describe as 'very able' or 'gifted' or 'talented'. Write down a few words, phrases or sentences you would use to explain to someone else why you selected that particular child and what special attributes you jotted down. A spider diagram may be a convenient format for you to represent your ideas (Figure 1.1).

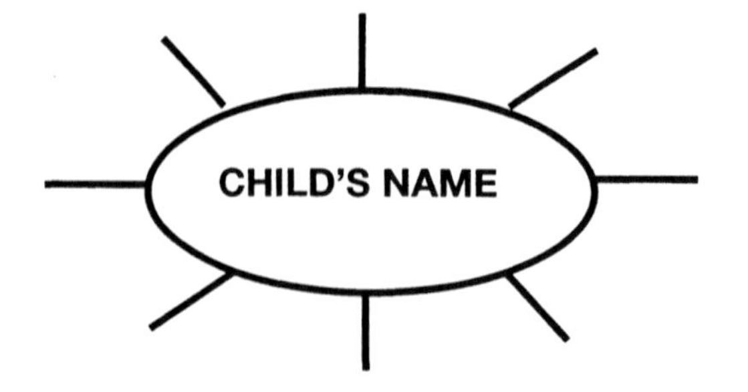

Figure 1.1 Recording 'gifted' attributes'

When you have completed the recording, share it with someone who knows the child to see if that person agrees with your perceptions. If you are doing this as a part of an in-service session, it would be very interesting to compare the list with that of others to see if there are similarities in the descriptions. Quite often I find that this exercise highlights the complexity of identification of gifted children and how difficult it is to make any generalisations. When we do this exercise with large numbers of teachers, one remarkable aspect I have noticed many times is that a significantly higher number of boys are selected. In the absence of any research evidence to offer explanations, we can only speculate on the reasons for this. What do you think may be the reasons?

When groups of teachers are engaged in the above exercise, one item which always crops up for discussion is the use of terminology. Who are we talking about? We use different terms to describe highly able children: *able, very able, exceptionally able, gifted, talented, bright* and *intelligent* are some of them. There is a common perception that by the term 'gifted' we mean children of exceptional ability and as a result I have often heard teachers say, *'but we haven't got any really gifted children in our school, we just have some bright children'*. The term 'gifted' is sometimes used to refer to children with very high IQ scores. From this perspective a gifted child is one with an IQ of 130 or more, by definition. I use the term 'gifted' in this book to refer to higher ability pupils, and for all practical purposes of provision I use our continuum model as can be shown in Figure 1.2.

Able → **more able** → **exceptionally able**

Figure 1.2 The ability continuum

Case studies

Although every child is unique in the way she or he demonstrates high ability and there are as many differences as similarities between them, I have included five case studies here of children who have either worked with me or were closely studied when they were referred to me. The reader is invited to study these cases. The intention is to facilitate reflection on the complexities of dealing with issues of giftedness. It is possible that these case studies will remind you of children in your classroom. I have provided a set of questions at the end of each case study for the reader to consider. It may be more fruitful to discuss these with a colleague or a friend. Try to consider the questions and write down your responses on a piece of paper. During in-service sessions, I encourage groups of teachers to imagine having these children in their classrooms and suggest what they would do with them.

Case study 1: James

James is five years old. His mother wrote to me a few weeks ago and told me she was *'at her wit's end'* trying to figure out what she should be doing with her son. The following profile was constructed from a two-page letter she sent me prior to arranging a meeting with her and James.

James has been very bright from an early age. He has always enjoyed watching television and the programme *Countdown* is a particular favourite. He walked early and could speak very well for his age and had a fascination for numbers. Around age 2, he taught himself to spell a number of words and could put a complex jigsaw puzzle together without any help. As he got older, before he was three, he would study a TV guide and mark what he would like to watch. He is still addicted to TV, resulting in the adults not being able to watch it very much. From age 2, he was like *a sponge absorbing all the information* he could from his surroundings. His conversations include the relative sizes of different fractions. He likes playing *Game Boy* and not much else.

James' mother says that she has some problems with him. He does not particularly like going to bed. He keeps pushing the boundaries by asking for 'five minutes more' every time. When he is finally in bed and if you sneak in to have a look, he is often reading a book. Harry Potter is a particular favourite.

James has a very caring teacher; she is willing to do anything. The school had warned the mother that there was very little they could do for him. He is getting frustrated when assigned work, which was 'easy' for him but was found 'very challenging' by most of the other children in the class.

Questions

- What indicators of high ability do you detect in James?
- If you were talking to James' class teacher, what advice would you give her?
- Would you recommend moving James up to a class where his intellectual needs may be met more adequately?
- What structures may be put in place for catering for the needs of children like James who show exceptional ability?
- How do you think other children of his age would react to him when he talks about topics which are beyond their understanding?
- Would you design an individual learning programme for him?
- How would you integrate him with the rest of the class?

Case study 2: Natalie

Natalie is seven years old. She is bright. She is one of the first ones to finish work. She is a neat worker and conforms to all the rules in the class. Natalie's mother recently heard that in a neighbouring school they have a 'gifted and talented' programme and very bright infants are allowed to attend a special maths club after school, and she wants to know why Natalie's school does not have a programme like that. She believes that Natalie is 'gifted' and she deserves better provision. Natalie's teacher and classroom assistant agree that she is bright, but not exceptional. According to her teacher, the work offered to Natalie within the classroom was felt to be adequate for her ability. This does not please her mother who is making arrangements for her to be assessed independently by a psychologist and if she *'comes out as gifted'* in the test she will then *'take this up further'.*

Questions

- What are your initial reactions to this case study?
- What use should the school make of the psychologist's report when it is presented?
- How could schools in the neighbouring area pool their resources and offer enrichment sessions?
- How would you select children for out-of-hours activities?

Case study 3: John

John attends a school in the Midlands. The following profile is constructed from his headteacher's letter. John is six years old and is working with a class of seven- to eight-year-olds at the moment. He is socially immature but asks many interesting questions. He enjoys talking to the teacher and would like to share his ideas with her more often. His special strength is mathematics. In fact, he is an outstanding mathematician. He is able to solve problems quite intuitively, sometimes giving answers without writing them down. He understands the 24-hour clock and can generalise rules during investigative work. The headteacher says that in his 30 years of teaching he has never met a child with higher ability in mathematics than John.

But everything is not as rosy as it seems. John has very poor coordination. His writing skills are not well developed and, as a result, he hates writing. He finds it difficult to accept imperfection of any sort and would rather avoid producing any work at all.

One option the school considered was to move John up to a Year 5 class.

Questions

- In what aspects does John demonstrate special strengths?
- What factors need to be taken into account when considering provision for him?
- Does moving him up to Year 5 offer a sensible solution?
- If you were designing an education plan for John, what form would it take?
- Is John gifted?

Case study 4: Ahmed

In 1994, I had the privilege to know and work with Ahmed who was featured in a BBC documentary entitled *Two Clever by Half.* Ahmed was six years old when his story was filmed. He was one of four children in his family. Ahmed liked his nursery school, but he did not like his infant school. When he was asked why he did not like his school his answer was that there was *'a lot of stuff to play with, but I wanted to learn too'.* He had a passion for learning. Having failed to find a school which would meet his needs, Ahmed's mother decided to educate him at home. She taught him for most of the time and occasionally paid for private tuition by saving money from the earnings of her husband who was a road sweeper. Ahmed never played with other children outside his home, which was on a council estate. Ahmed's IQ was tested and found to be very high, placing him at a high position in the 'gifted' range. Ahmed excelled in mathematics, story-writing and in science. He produced stories with a mature style and could discuss topics such as gravity and weightlessness. His mother wanted him to do GCSE when he reached age 8.

Questions

- Why do you think that the schools near where Ahmed lived felt they could not meet his needs?
- What are Ahmed's special needs?
- What do you think about Ahmed's mother's wish to enter him for GCSE at age 8?
- If Ahmed's parents applied to your school, what procedures would you follow from the time of application to the time he joined the school?
- What are your feelings about gifted children being educated at home?

Case study 5: Matthew

Five-year-old Matthew's teacher told me that one morning he came into the classroom and told her, '*I am not going to do any work for you any more*'. When she asked why, he explained that he thinks he does more work than anyone else and gets less '*choosing time*' than anyone else. He explained further: '*When I finish some work, you give me some more, or ask me to copy my work out neatly. I am fed up with it*.' He said he liked choosing time the best when he could pretend to be a pilot or an astronaut or build a bridge or an aeroplane. Although Matthew's teacher appreciated his honest remarks she said she was 'upset and ashamed' that she was doing nothing to encourage his creativity and imagination and in fact was '*punishing him for being very clever*'.

Another time, Matthew pointed out that he was always the one who '*waited*' in the class. He was always told to 'wait' until the others had finished, 'wait' until the teacher had seen all the others, wait to be picked when he put his hand up in the English lesson when he wanted to tell his story to everyone about pretending to be a raindrop.

Questions

- Do you have children who 'wait' for other children to finish?
- What do you do with those children who already know what you are going to teach the rest of the class?
- Is 'play' and 'choosing' time beneficial to very able children?
- Would you expect Matthew's kind of honesty from older children? What might older children do instead, to avoid being given extra work when all the assigned tasks are completed?

Considering the above case studies should highlight the challenge facing a teacher in both identifying gifted children and making appropriate provision for them.

Summary

In this chapter, I have tried to provide the background for the contents of this book. The initial consideration of the importance of identification of special abilities of children and the need for appropriate provision permeates throughout the book. Recent developments in gifted education in England and Wales, which provides a backdrop for the contents of this book, were discussed. Government initiatives for enhancing educational opportunities for all young children's education were referred to in setting up a framework for provision. Five case studies of children, who are considered by their parents or teachers as 'gifted', were presented in order to facilitate reflection on the challenges facing schools and individual teachers in their efforts to make effective provision for younger higher ability children.

Two issues are worthy of your attention. First, you may wish to think about the challenging task of identifying 5 to 10 per cent of 'gifted and talented' children in your class. Many schools are already doing this. Second, consider whether the whole issue of identification of gifted children creates any particular dilemmas in the context of children aged 4–7.

2 Identifying younger gifted children

Let us consider some scenarios of younger children who could be described as gifted and see how their teachers responded to them. Robert's class of four-year-olds were told that the school was closed for teachers' *inset* on Monday. His imagination came to life and he started telling his class teacher that he hoped she would see lots of beetles, butterflies and other insects and have an enjoyable day. He insisted on finding out more about insects at home from the Internet for her. The next day he came up to her with an impressive list of specimens she might see in the insect museum. Although it did not take her long to work out that Robert misunderstood 'inset' for 'insect', she was unwilling to curb Robert's enthusiasm and his initiative. Robert is very articulate. He takes the initiative and exhibits leadership at an early age. He is lucky to have a teacher who acknowledges his abilities and encourages him. This is not always the case. Seven-year-old Anna, who worked with me at the University, told me that her teacher tore up her homework – a story – because Anna had not used all the words she had been instructed to; she had used too many scientific words such as 'water molecules' and 'water-cycle' in her creative writing entitled 'The story of a raindrop'. Her research at home and initiative had not been rewarded so positively. Most of us know the story of the famous mathematician – Gauss – who worked out the question: If you add up all the numbers from 1 to 100 what is the total? in a matter of a few minutes, to the surprise of all his classmates and his teacher. His mathematical ability was easily spotted. Finally, one vivid memory I have of a seven-year-old is a follows:

David: Can I stop working for a few minutes and tell you something? Can you keep a secret? It really is top secret.

V: I will keep it a secret if you like. Go on, tell me.

David: Well, I was tested and my mum found out that I have an IQ of 160. She says that makes me severely gifted. She doesn't want me to tell anyone.

V: Why is that?

David: In our school they, the other kids, will tease me and call me all sorts of names.

V: So what do you do with all that brain then?

David: I have lessons in the evening, I will take my GCSE in two years' time.

After telling me about his secrets including the one about the twilight lesson, David settled down and appeared relieved to have told someone about what may have been disturbing him for some time. When I asked him why he did not share this information with his teacher, he replied: *'She hasn't got any time, she has to sort out all the trouble-makers.'*

As explained in Chapter 1, the education of gifted children has not always received the attention it deserves until recently. Sadly, many adults believe in the myth that gifted children can look after themselves and that they are privileged in every way. It may be true that they learn faster, but they have their own needs. For example, their special strengths and talents need to be acknowledged and they need to be offered intellectually challenging learning experiences.

The aim of this chapter is to take a close look at ways in which we can identify children's talents. A good starting point is to quote Estelle Morris the Schools Minister, who expressed the government's objective clearly:

> The government is committed to improving educational standards for all children ... to help the most able achieve their full potential and to develop a clear national strategy to improve the education of gifted and talented children.
>
> (DfEE 1998: 1)

Before we discuss ways of identifying children's special abilities, I would like to stress that we need to take account of both high achievement and potential. In all situations discussed above, we can see how some of them had a fair deal when it came to their teachers responding to their needs and others did not receive treatment which was entirely fair.

Identification of gifted children

Identifying gifted children is a complex process. In Chapter 1, I highlighted that the term – gifted – alone creates difficulties for many teachers. During in-service sessions, teachers have often said that they have benefited from a consideration of different perspectives on ability. They feel that an enhancement of their own understanding of aspects of ability helps them to be aware of the challenges facing them, and supports them in making valid and effective assessments of their pupils' abilities. In the past few years there has been a shift from viewing ability as a single dimensional measure to it being a multi-dimensional, broader concept. In the following section I will present a brief summary of international perspectives on the nature of giftedness and the implications of the various models for classroom practice. Readers are invited to read the original sources, given in the reference section, for a more comprehensive discussion of these.

Defining giftedness

First, try a task. Write a few statements you would use to describe attributes of a 'gifted' child. Then compare your list with the following list of attributes offered by a group of teachers who attended an in-service session. Gifted children:

- are those who have high intelligence; they will have high IQs
- achieve higher levels in SATs
- usually have abilities in mathematics and science
- know everything before you teach them
- are very creative
- are very articulate and confident
- are the ones the teacher feels guilty about not spending much time with them.

Each of these statements has a particular story to tell. The given range of attributes also shows the difficulty in defining giftedness. After reading the following section, where I have attempted to provide an overview of theoretical perspectives, I hope that readers will be able to construct their own theories and put them into practical use.

Intelligent quotient

When people refer to high IQ scores they are referring to results obtained by psychometric testing. IQ tests provide a single score measurement of ability. IQ tests are designed to test potential and are viewed by many as a useful means of selecting a 'gifted' population. As Figure 2.1 shows, the average score is 100 and the area on the extreme right (from 130 upwards) represents the 'gifted' population. IQs of 150 and 160 are meant to show exceptional potential to learn. It should be noted that the score of 100 is the average for the individual child's age group. A child with an IQ above 130 is more than two standard deviations above the average for the child's age groups. The IQ is normally distributed with a standard deviation of 15. The bar chart (Figure 2.1) is an approximate form of the continuous, smooth, normal curve with mean $\mu = 100$ and standard deviation $\sigma = 15$ (μ is pronounced mu and σ is pronounced sigma).

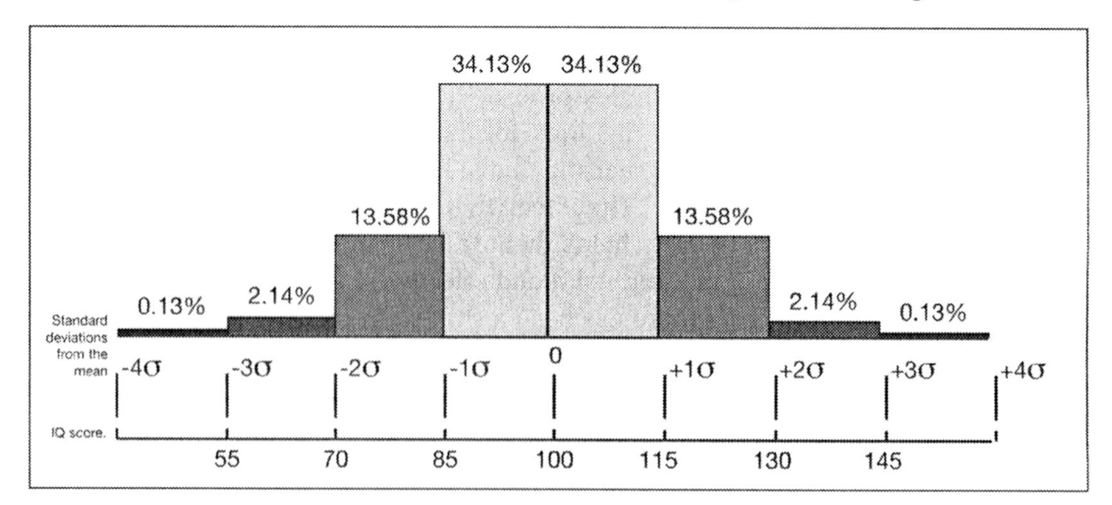

Figure 2. 1: Distribution of ability

Early definitions of ability were based on a measure of intelligence quotient described as the 'general intelligence factor' (the g factor), indicating pupils' ability to reason and make connections. IQ tests are quite often used for selection purposes by some schools. Psychologists use IQ tests for diagnostic purposes.

Although it is accepted that IQ tests serve some useful purposes, their use as an exclusive means of identification is questioned by many. Critics point out that many factors can affect IQ test results. The way a child feels on the day of the test, or even the way the test is carried out, can influence the final score. In addition, a child who may be creative or is a divergent thinker may not do well in an IQ test. Also, many educationists and psychologists believe that a single measure of intelligence does not acknowledge the diverse talents, aptitudes and abilities of pupils. They believe that a broader concept of giftedness, assessing a range of abilities, is likely to lead to an enhanced quality of provision for gifted children.

Multi-dimensional identification

A departure from the single dimensional measuring of abilities in the USA was in evidence at the time of the publication of the Marland Report (1972) which proposed six categories of gifted and talented children who were to be identified by 'virtue of outstanding abilities and capable performances' in these areas. The listed areas were:

1. general intellectual ability
2. specific academic aptitude
3. creative or productive thinking
4. leadership ability
5. visual or performing arts
6. psychomotor ability.

In the UK, a model proposed by Ogilvie (1973) is not dissimilar in the message it sends: we need to consider a range of talents and abilities in children. Six categories of giftedness were listed:

1. leadership
2. high intelligence
3. artistic talent
4. creativity
5. physical talent
6. mechanical ingenuity.

Howard Gardner's theory of Multiple Intelligences

Howard Gardner's (1983, 1993) theory of Multiple Intelligences won international recognition and acquired wide acceptance by the education community because of the way Gardner persuades many that ability shows itself in a variety of ways and that children possess multiple talents which need to be recognised. Since his theory was launched, many educational programmes around the world, based on his views, have been devised. The theory of Multiple Intelligences describes ability in domain-specific terms. On the basis of his work with prodigies and those with partial brain damage, he proposed seven intelligences, acknowledging that there are more. Two more intelligences – naturalist and existential – have been added since. Gardner defines an intelligence as the ability to solve problems or fashion products that are valued in one or more cultural settings. The first seven intelligences proposed are:

1 Linguistic intelligence (language)
2 Logical-mathematical intelligence (mathematics and sciences)
3 Bodily kinaesthetic intelligence (physical)
4 Musical intelligence (music and rhythm)
5 Spatial intelligence (space)
6 Interpersonal intelligence (interpersonal skills, leadership skills)
7 Intrapersonal intelligence (ability to reflect on oneself).

The perspective on domain-specific ability, put forward by Gardner, appeals to many educationists for a number of reasons. First, because it acknowledges children's multiple talents. A child may demonstrate one or more of the intelligences or show outstanding performance in one area. Second, there is no ranking of the intelligences, thus encouraging us to celebrate all abilities. Teachers with whom I have worked have often felt comfortable with this model, as it provides a framework for a flexible identification system. Consideration of specific abilities also suggests ways forward with regard to provision. Gardner himself recommends that creative and stimulating programmes and resources should be provided to enhance the development of these intelligences.

Support for subject-specific models of provision has gained much support among leading experts in curriculum provision for able pupils. In a clear and convincing voice, Van Tassel-Baska (1992), a leading expert in the USA on curriculum provision for gifted pupils, lists the reasons for moving to a content-based instructional model for the gifted. Van Tassel-Baska's arguments are both logical and practical:

> Schools are organised by content areas, and to deviate significantly from these areas is to be outside a predominant organisational pattern that aids communication on gifted issues within the school system. It also provides the natural context for planning the curriculum, because of school systems, even those with self-contained programmes for the gifted, are obliged to show mastery of basic skills for gifted in these subject matter areas, the impact of programmes for the gifted is limited by ignoring content.
>
> (Van Tassel-Baska 1992: 2)

Van Tassel-Baska argues that knowledge at a social level is also organised in discipline-specific ways. She puts forward arguments for this view by citing the example of Nobel prizes being awarded in specific disciplines.

In Britain, guidelines for the Foundation Stage include subject-specific guidance, the National Curriculum is set in specific subject areas, we have a national literacy and numeracy programme and, of course, we have SATs which assess children's competence in discrete subjects. These suggest that we should address subject-specific provision.

I believe that Gardner's theory of Multiple Intelligences offers a sound and practical framework for assessing young children's particular abilities, especially in the first years of schooling, because of the flexibility it offers in making decisions. As I feel that his theoretical perspective is worth considering when we make judgements about giftedness, I will provide brief explanations of these seven intelligences. These are my interpretations of Gardner's (1993) views. For exemplification of these intelligences, I have used examples of well-known people, used by Gardner, who have made significant contributions to their societies.

Linguistic intelligence

Children who are linguistically gifted appreciate the order, meanings and rhythm of words. They enjoy the challenge of decoding the rules of grammar, inventing new language and playing with words. They have extensive vocabulary and enjoy communicating. Gardner uses T. S. Eliot as an example of someone who possesses this gift. Eliot created a magazine called *Fireside* when he was just ten years old. In a three-day period during a winter holiday, he created ten complete issues of the magazine.

Musical intelligence

Those who possess this intelligence are sensitive to rhythm, pitch and timbre, and appreciate timing and tone. They enjoy both creating and listening to music. They can often recognise melodies with stunning accuracy. Yehudi Menuhin is an example of someone with this kind of talent, whose remarkable gift for music manifested itself even before he touched a violin.

Spatial intelligence

A person who is able to perceive the visual world and to make representations of parts of it may possesses this intelligence. Pablo Picasso is an example of someone who possessed this intelligence. The ability to create mental images and use them in unfamiliar circumstances is also a feature of this intelligence.

Logical-mathematical intelligence

The use of logic, deduction and reasoning is characteristic of this intelligence. Those who exhibit this kind of intelligence are good problem-solvers. They also display powers of categorising, calculating, hypothesising, experimenting and developing arguments. Einstein is an example of someone who possessed this intelligence.

Bodily kinaesthetic intelligence

A person with this intelligence will have the ability to use his or her body to express an emotion (as in 'dance') or to play a game (as in a sport) or to create a new product (as in inventing) – all evidence of resourceful use of one's body. Martha Graham, the dancer and choreographer, is an example of someone who possessed this high degree of bodily kinaesthetic intelligence.

Interpersonal intelligence

Gardner describes people with this intelligence who have the ability to notice distinctions between people, contrasts in their moods, temperaments, motivations and intentions. Such people are likely to be more empathetic, and more effective leaders, organisers and managers. Mahatma Gandhi who won the respect of millions of people for his influence with non-violent protests is an example of someone who possessed this kind of intelligence.

Intrapersonal intelligence

Those who have good insights about their own emotions and are capable of labelling and discriminating between them as well as drawing on them to guide their own behaviour have interpersonal intelligence. People with this kind of intelligence have a heightened awareness of their own strengths and weaknesses. Sigmund Freud is cited as an example of someone who had this kind of intelligence.

Gardner has added other forms of intelligence to his list. These are not included in this book, as I feel the original seven offer a sound enough framework for what I suggest as a basis for identifying children's strengths.

It is possible that while reading these descriptions you were trying to match the seven intelligences to famous personalities from the past and present whom you know. Try thinking about the children in your class and consider what intelligences they exhibit. Then ask whether children in your classroom get opportunities to demonstrate the different kinds of intelligence. How Gardner's intelligences may be used as an initial checklist for identifying children's individual strengths is discussed later in this chapter.

In terms of the definition offered by the DfEE as referred to in Chapter 1 – children being described as 'gifted' in academic subjects and as 'talented' if their abilities are in creative and artistic subjects – Gardner's Multiple Intelligences provide a good starting point for identifying gifted and talented children. Linguistic, spatial and logical-mathematical intelligences are suggestive of academic excellence while the other intelligences may be referred to as talents. A word of caution here. It would be very unwise to match the children exclusively to certain intelligences or to think that they may possess one single intelligence. Most children are likely to show combinations of the intelligences.

Renzulli's Three-ring Model

A model proposed by Renzulli (1986) suggests three factors as important in the identification of a pupil's abilities. They are: ***above-average ability, creativity*** and ***task commitment*** (see Figure 2.2). Renzulli considers that all three aspects are important in the identification and development of abilities. These three elements provide a framework for making sure that talents are nurtured and developed. A practical and useful task which arises out of this model is to think about how we ensure that we can help children to have task commitment and how creativity can be encouraged. People who have made significant contributions in various fields were known for their single-mindedness, task commitment and persistence. Encouragement to pursue one's own interests would be a necessary condition for realising a person's true potential.

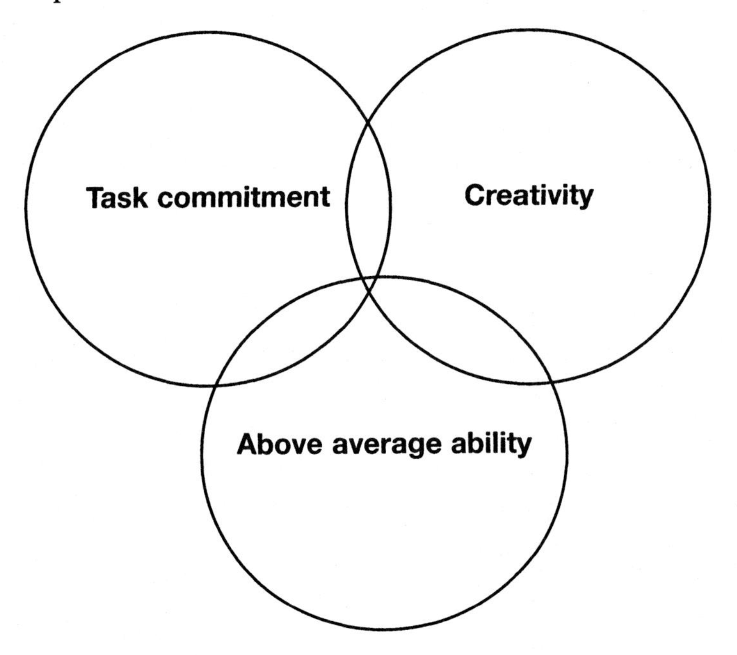

Figure 2.2 Renzulli's Three-ring Model

Sternberg (1986) from Yale University is also among those who have put forward theories on ability which go beyond a single measure of intelligence. His *Triarchic theory* defines intelligence in terms on how it is applied to real situations. For Sternberg, indicators of giftedness are provided by the ability to make the best use of the environment. Again, this has implications for both identification of and provision for gifted children.

Finally, it is very important to remember that the development of ability does not happen at a fixed rate at fixed times. This has particular relevance in the first years of children's schooling. Silverman (1993) describes the development of the cognitive, emotional and physical factors as 'asynchronous' development occurring at different rates, and the more gifted a child is the more pronounced the unevenness could be.

Silverman (1992, quoted in Morelock and Morrison 1996), sends a strong message to all those involved in educating young gifted children: *Asynchrony in the gifted means a 'lack of synchronicity in the rates of cognitive, emotional and physical development'.*

She adds that the lack of synchronicity creates inner tension, as when a five-year-old child perceives a horse through an eight-year-old's eyes, but cannot replicate the horse in clay with her five-year-old fingers. This can lead to frustration.

Principles into practice

Having considered various theoretical principles, let us now explore ways in which a practising teacher can recognise and acknowledge younger children's various abilities. First, think for a moment and try to construct a concept map or a web diagram of the various perspectives on ability to enhance your own understanding of issues.

Challenges and concerns

Identification of gifted children of any age is a complex task and it may be particularly challenging with regard to making assessments of younger children's special strengths. So what are the difficulties, especially with regard to identification of younger gifted children? Consider the following dilemmas and concerns expressed by practising teachers:

- One way of identifying gifted children – using cognitive tests – does not seem very practical with four- and five-year-olds, and even if we have test scores for younger children they are likely to change at a faster rate than those for older children.
- Younger children do not develop in predetermined sequences and any information we may have will be only a snapshot for that particular time.
- Performance of younger children in tests and results of observation schedules can be influenced by factors such as pre-school experiences, home background and the nature of their physical environment; for example, the presence of books and other stimulation.
- It is too early to label children as gifted and non-gifted.
- The mismatch between cognitive and physical development in younger children is often more pronounced and this can make identification difficult.
- There is a serious lack of in-service support and resources for infant and nursery teachers on aspects of gifted education.

Identification of even older children is not straight forward. Eyre (2001) points out that the creation of a 5 to 10 per cent gifted and talented population in secondary schools, which is a requirement from the DfES, 'has been the most problematic aspect' of the government's Excellence in Cities gifted and talented strand. She adds that the 'tension' relating to identification is even more 'magnified' in primary schools. For all the reasons given in the previous section, the identification and creation of lists of gifted children need to be flexible, and adults who make decisions about children's capabilities need to be open-minded and more vigilant.

My own thinking is that in the context of the first years of schooling, it makes more sense to gather information on children's multiple strengths before creating a list of 'gifted' pupils. From the information gathered, a list of both the gifted and talented (see DfEE definition in Chapter 1, p. 3) will emerge. Again, I emphasise that a list of children's interests and strengths is likely to help teachers to plan more appropriate provision for their children.

A case for early identification

Although the whole issue of identification is strewn with difficulties, I think it is important that we support the notion of early identification of gifted children, whether they demonstrate all-round abilities or show specific strengths. I put forward the following arguments to justify the above statement:

- The first years of schooling constitute a very important stage in children's lives when interests are developed and attitudes formed. We cannot afford to make mistakes at this very crucial stage of their development.
- Mastery of facts, skills and conceptual understanding at this stage is important to support a robust framework of knowledge. Gaps at this stage can lead to serious underachievement later in their education.
- Research has shown that high-quality early years programmes can make a significant contribution to children's attitudes to learning and in their achievement (Sylva 1994).
- Brain function research (Rutter and Rutter 1992) suggests that we can make a significant change in children's learning potential in the first few years of their lives.

In order to create a reliable and useful record of children's strengths, we need to amass information about them from all available sources as well as collecting and using the information systematically. It is useful to remember the three Ms when gathering information. For any information gathering to be effective, the process should involve **M**ultiple sources, it should be **M**anageable and it should be collected **M**ethodically.

In the following sections, a number of strategies for collecting and recording information on children's strengths and abilities are presented. Many of these strategies may already be in operation, but may just need a little more organisation. I hope that the end result of achieving a fair, flexible and sensible strategy for identifying gifted children will justify the efforts.

Strategies for identifying children's strengths

Involving parents

Involving parents in the identification of children's special strengths is important at all phases of schooling. In the first years of schooling it is even more important. Most parents know about what their children can do well before they start school.

Although some parents may have exaggerated views of their children's abilities, I find that in many cases their observations are accurate and very reliable. I know parents who have told me that somehow they knew there was something 'special' about their children before they were even two years old. Quite often very young gifted children recognise shop signs, teach themselves to read, have a fascination for numbers, show interest in adult conversations and may get involved in discussing topics with adults. So, how can we enlist parents' help in the identification process? One simple starting point is to provide a space in the first application form before the child starts school, where parents are asked to list any special talents or strengths they have noticed. Specific questions can also be asked at the time of the interview. I have seen in many school admission forms a space asking parents to list any problems; perhaps it is time that we ask if their children exhibit any special talents too. Any recording of strengths should also be followed up at the interview stage. A simple letter (Figure 2.3) or a questionnaire (Figure 2.4) which you are free to copy or adapt, would be very beneficial. At the university we regularly do this prior to enrolling children for special programmes and find the information from parents extremely useful.

Some schools send a short leaflet describing some salient points of the schools' policy for nurturing special abilities. Parents may also be offered a workshop, again explaining what the school is trying to do and asking for their contributions to be mentors, to provide leadership in specialised areas or with extra visits to places of interest. Parents are also in a position to notice their children's special abilities and behaviour which may not always be exhibited in the school. Parents need to be encouraged to share this information with the child's teacher at any time in the school year.

Teacher observation

Teacher observation, along with information from parents, would provide an effective way of identifying children's abilities, as teachers do spend a significant time with their children in the classroom. Perhaps I need to qualify the above statement by saying that teachers will observe excellence in children's output only if they provide conditions where children can respond to stimulating and challenging activities. For example, it is unlikely that a teacher would identify mathematical giftedness if the work provided is repetitive and not cognitively demanding. A child cannot show high levels of problem-solving skills or application of logic if most of the work on offer is in the form of sums. Similarly, linguistically talented children will exhibit their strengths only if motivating opportunities are provided for them in the form of wordtasks and creative writing. Here are some of the ways in which a teacher can collect information.

Interviewing the child

One of the ways in which a teacher can find out about the child is to conduct a short interview with a child early in the year. It does not need to be long and you only need to record information which highlights any special interests. Most children respond

HELP ME TO IDENTIFY YOUR CHILD'S SPECIAL STRENGTHS

Child's Name ....

Dear Parent / Carer

We believe that as parents and carers you notice your children's special strengths at home. Sometimes children do not show these strengths in school. In order to help us to identify and nurture your child's strengths, I request you to complete the child's talent survey and the special ability questionnaire. In the blank space provided, please feel free to add any special moments or examples of your child's hobbies or achievements. Any photographs or examples of work given to me with the completed questionnaire will be safely returned.

Your Child's Teacher

Figure 2.3 Parents' letter for talent identification

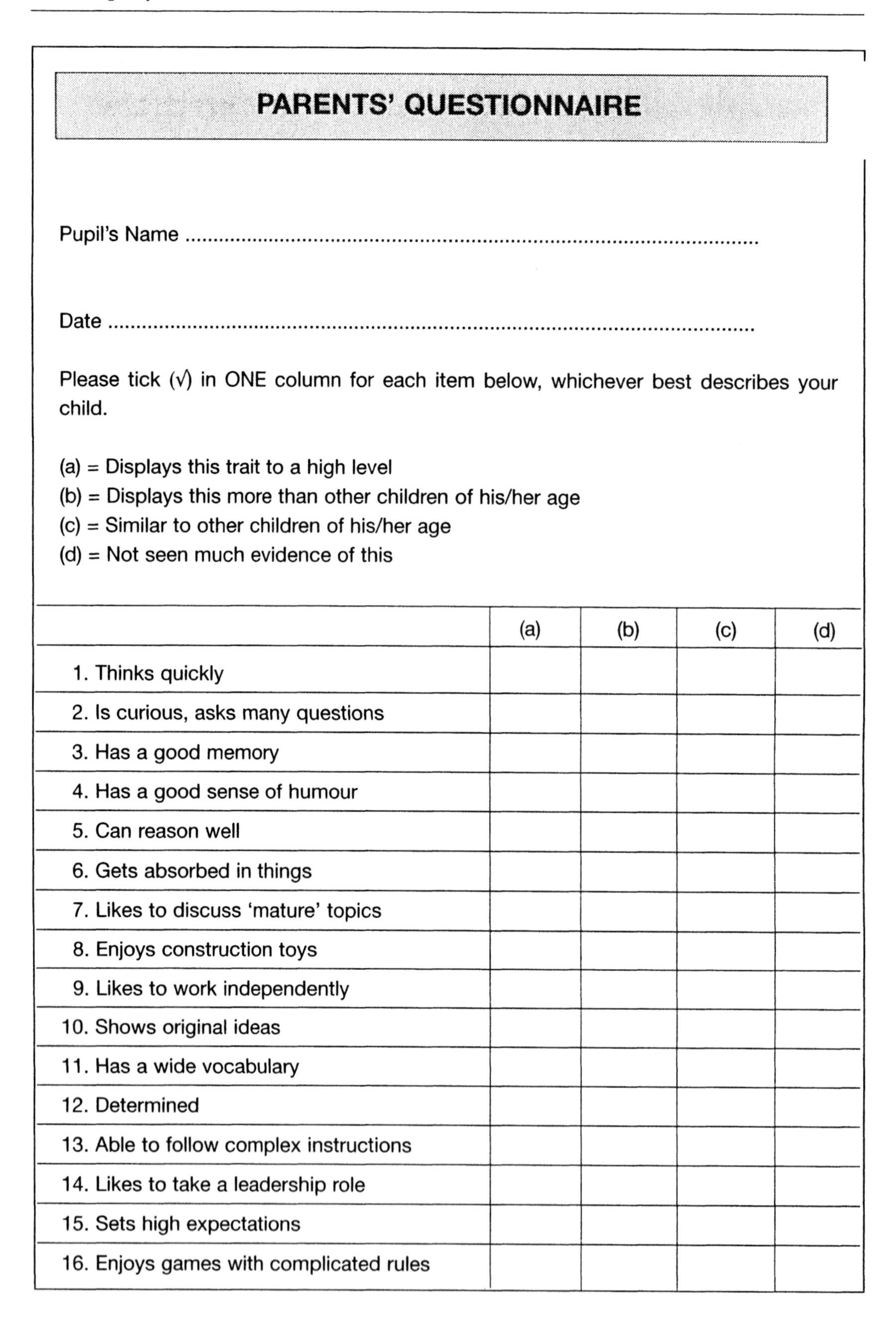

PARENTS' QUESTIONNAIRE

Pupil's Name ....

Date ....

Please tick (√) in ONE column for each item below, whichever best describes your child.

(a) = Displays this trait to a high level
(b) = Displays this more than other children of his/her age
(c) = Similar to other children of his/her age
(d) = Not seen much evidence of this

	(a)	(b)	(c)	(d)
1. Thinks quickly				
2. Is curious, asks many questions				
3. Has a good memory				
4. Has a good sense of humour				
5. Can reason well				
6. Gets absorbed in things				
7. Likes to discuss 'mature' topics				
8. Enjoys construction toys				
9. Likes to work independently				
10. Shows original ideas				
11. Has a wide vocabulary				
12. Determined				
13. Able to follow complex instructions				
14. Likes to take a leadership role				
15. Sets high expectations				
16. Enjoys games with complicated rules				

Figure 2.4 Parents' talent questionnaire

to this kind of special attention very positively. You could ask children to bring something from home which they would like to talk about, or you may ask some structured questions, such as:

- What do you like doing when you are not doing school work?
- What are your interests?
- What would you say you are very good at?
- If you could start a special club, what would the club members do?

Tape-recording these interviews would enable you to listen without having to take notes; only relevant information would then need to be written down. Carrying out an interview not only provides the teacher with information, it also makes the child feel valued. In addition, focusing on talents sends the important message to all concerned that talents and excellence are valued in your classroom.

Developing talent portfolios

A portfolio is a collection of children's work or any kind of evidence of special strengths. It must be developed in partnership with the child, both the teacher and the child including the best examples of a range of children's tangible outcomes. The pieces selected for inclusion may have been done either in school or at home. Children can be asked to justify the reasons for selecting a piece of work for inclusion. This could be written down by either the child or the teacher and this process alone encourages reflection and evaluation. Pieces of work, photographs of models, copies of certificates and accounts of hobbies or activities can be included. As well as providing evidence of special strengths and achievement, talent portfolios help:

- the teacher to plan appropriate activities to support the child's special aptitudes;
- to keep an ongoing partnership with home and parents;
- make children feel that their gifts are valued which helps to develop their self-esteem;
- to evaluate children's progress.

Where the portfolios are stored and whether to have a two-part portfolio – one for the teacher to keep the information collected from parents, the close observation notes or commentary, and the other for the child to be totally responsible for – should be considered. The second part may contain pieces selected by the child with help from parents or teachers. It is up to each individual teacher to decide these matters according to school policy. Portfolio entries need not be restricted to the class teacher's comments. Other teachers, classroom assistants and helpers can also provide appropriate commentary. As I believe that a child's portfolio can play an important role in both identification and provision, I have included more aspects of keeping portfolios in Chapter 4.

Use of attribute checklists

Schools and sometimes LEAs use general attributes checklists for assessing gifted pupils. These checklists can provide initial indicators of pupils' abilities and are often described as 'useful' by many teachers. However, caution will need to be exercised in relying on checklists which generalise attributes in gifted children. Freeman (1998) advocates caution about the use of checklists – that they can be confusing, misleading and inaccurate is worth taking into account. She provides a research-based checklist. The list includes the following criteria exhibited by very able pupils:

- Memory and knowledge – excellent memory and use of information.
- Self-regulation – they know how they learn best and can monitor their learning.
- Speed of thought – they may spend longer on planning but then reach decisions more speedily.
- Dealing with problems – they add to the information, spot what is irrelevant and get to the essentials quickly.
- Flexibility – although their thinking is usually more organised than other children's they can see and adopt alternative solutions to learning and problem-solving.
- Preference for complexity – they tend to make games and tasks more complex to increase interest.
- They have an exceptional ability to concentrate at will and for longer periods of time from an earlier age.
- Early symbolic activity – they may speak, read and write early.

Many of the characteristics listed above were also found by Koshy and Casey (1997b, 2000) through their observation and notes kept on several hundreds of children who attended programmes designed and run by the authors between 1992 and 2000. Some of the characteristics exhibited by the children which are of practical significance for teachers are as follows:

- They showed dislike of repetitive work.
- Quite often they shared the anxiety they felt about other children not accepting their high ability and, as a result, not being chosen as 'friends'.
- If interested in a project or activity, many resented imposed time constraints.
- They were often creative in offering solutions, but unsure if the creative solutions would be appreciated by the teacher.
- They chose unusual methods of working which they were not always able to explain.

Checklists can provide teachers with an initial framework for assessing children's abilities which can then be followed up using a more systematic framework of assessment. Readers should find the following checklist provided by Silverman (1993), which includes both intellectual and personality characteristics of gifted children, very useful for both identification and for the counselling needs of gifted children.

INTELLECTUAL CHARACTERISTICS

- exceptional reasoning ability
- intellectual curiosity
- rapid learning rate
- facility with abstraction
- complex thought processes
- vivid imagination
- early moral concern
- passion for learning
- powers of concentration
- analytical thinking
- divergent thinking/creativity
- keen sense of justice
- capacity for reflection.

PERSONALITY CHARACTERISTICS

- insightfulness
- need to understand
- need for mental stimulation
- perfectionism
- need for precision/logic
- excellent sense of humour
- sensitivity/empathy
- intensity
- perseverance
- acute self-awareness
- non-conformity
- questioning of rules/authority
- tendency towards introversion.

It should be interesting to think about the children in your class and judge if they exhibit any of the above attributes.

Using Gardners' Multiple Intelligences checklist

Since Gardner put forward his theory of Multiple Intelligences many education programmes have ben devised on the basis of it. Gardner maintains that his theory was not formulated for any specific educational application and he insists that using his theories for educational assessment is not a fruitful idea. Instead, as he has shown through the school-based projects he has supported, his main emphasis is on providing opportunities for children to demonstrate their different strengths. Gardner explains his thinking behind an education project based on his theory – Project Spectrum – which was initiated by himself and his colleagues:

> Rather than devising yet another test battery, we created a rich environment – one called 'spectrum classroom ' – in which children would be comfortable. Our initial Spectrum site, a pre-school, was well stocked with material to activate the different intelligences, including specimens of nature, board games, artistic and musical materials, and areas for exercise, dance, and building. We assumed that children would find these material inviting, that they would interact with them regularly, and that they would reveal to us, by the richness and sophistication of their interactions, their particular array of intelligences. Hence the title Spectrum.
> (Gardner 1999: 136)

Gardner goes on to say that his approach rested on:

> an important principle. Rather than bringing children to the assessment ... we took assessment to the children. We created an environment with inviting resources and let the children demonstrate their spectra of intelligence in as natural a fashion as possible.

Gardner's Multiple Intellingences theory provides a framework for teachers to observe children's special strengths, as long as the opportunities are provided for them to demonstrate their abilities. I will deal with aspects of creating a rich learning environment, in much more detail, in Chapter 3. The following framework, (Figure 2.5) based on Gardner's Multiple Intelligences theory, may be helpful for observing children's special aptitudes. A school may be able to adapt this to suit the structure of their classroom practice. If a simpler version is preferred you may use the format given in Figure 2.6 where you would record and date any significant information in the space provided.

Using tests

At present young children are assessed using baseline tests at the start of schooling. This should provide some data on children's areas of strengths. All children in maintained schools are also assessed through standard tests (SATs), though not until they are aged seven. These often give indications of subject-specific ability, knowledge, speed of information-processing and problem-solving ability. Some schools use commercially produced assessment material to test children at different points in the school year. In some cases educational psychologists are invited to carry out IQ tests to assess the potential of students who are underachieving or those who have specific learning difficulties. The information collected during these tests can be useful in assessing potential ability in verbal reasoning and problem-solving skills. IQ tests may be useful predictors of examination success, but the scores are not likely to suggest specific ways of providing for pupils who have obtained high scores. Nevertheless, test results when used with other evidence of achievement add to the range of evidence of children's ability. All test results contribute to the ongoing profile of the child. However, tests should never replace the role of teacher observation because identification based on teacher observation enables us to take into account Howe's (1998) viewpoint (see p. 32).

OBSERVATION OF SPECIAL STRENGTHS BASED ON M.I. THEORY

Child's Name ....

Class Teacher ....

Tick the box(1–5) which closely matches your observation of the child's specific strengths. Do the checklist half-termly or termly. Add any comments on the grid marked General Comments.

(1) = Not observed this
(2) = Occasionally seen this
(3) = Usually observe this
(4) = Almost always observe this
(5) = No opportunity to observe this

LINGUISTIC INTELLIGENCE	**(1)**	**(2)**	**(3)**	**(4)**	**(5)**
1. Enjoys activities involving the use of words, spellings, memorising poems, and riddles.					
2. Enjoys discussions – factual and imaginative. Can verbalise ideas.					
3. Expresses ideas orally or in writing. Is a good storywriter or teller.					
4. Has an extensive vocabulary.					
5. Asks many questions.					
6. Shows interest in English and responds well to the challenge of other languages.					

LOGICAL–MATHEMATICAL INTELLIGENCE	**(1)**	**(2)**	**(3)**	**(4)**	**(5)**
1. Enjoys playing or working with number activities.					
2. Shows a good awareness of pattern and sequence.					
3. Can provide explanations and generalise in some form.					
4. Assembles puzzles with skill.					
5. Produces logical arguments.					
6. Sorts objects using different criteria and finds similarities and differences.					
7. Demonstrates problem-solving skills and shows skills in dealing with unfamiliar contexts.					
8. Is able to plan and describe steps in order and explain reasons.					

BODILY KINAESTHETIC INTELLIGENCE	**(1)**	**(2)**	**(3)**	**(4)**	**(5)**
1. Good motor skills: skipping, jumping, balances.					
2. Uses body with agility.					
3. Shows ability to master new physical skills.					
4. Enjoys touching and manipulating objects in order to learn about them.					
5. Shows aptitude with movements, e.g. dancing.					

MUSICAL INTELLIGENCE	(1)	(2)	(3)	(4)	(5)
1. Enjoys musical activities.					
2. Shows aptitude to reproduce new melodies or rhythm.					
3. Composes music patterns and melodies.					
4. Shows ability to identify musical instruments heard in musical compositions.					
5. Plays musical selections by ear or hums it melodically.					
6. Experiments with object to create different sounds.					

SPATIAL INTELLIGENCE	(1)	(2)	(3)	(4)	(5)
1. Shows aptitude for constructions and designs.					
2. Shows the ability to dismantle things and reassemble.					
3. Ability or organise and group objects.					
4. Demonstrates artistic flair: responds to texture, colour and pattern.					
5. Visualises details and perspectives.					

INTERPERSONAL INTELLIGENCE	(1)	(2)	(3)	(4)	(5)
1. Enjoys helping others.					
2. Shows a sense of fairness for members in a group and shows empathy.					
3. Shows leadership skills.					
4. Expresses feelings to others.					
5. Shows the need to meet own needs through other adults and peers.					
6. Participates in group activities.					
7. Builds relationships easily.					

INTRAPERSONAL INTELLIGENCE	(1)	(2)	(3)	(4)	(5)
1. Shows awareness of own strengths and weaknesses.					
2. Shows capability to be self-reflective and engages in self-evaluation.					
3. Shows self-confidence.					
4. Capable of laughing at oneself.					
5. Takes risks.					
6. Sticks to own beliefs.					
7. Shows ability to work independently.					
8. Shows persistence in self-selected activities.					

Figure 2.5 An observation framework based on Gardner's Mutiple Intelligences theory

COMMENTS: *(Add any particular examples or contexts where a certain strength was shown)* **Child's name** ....
• **Linguistic intelligence**
• **Logical-mathematical intelligence**
• **Bodily kinaesthetic intelligence**
• **Musical intelligence**
• **Spatial intelligence**
• **Interpersonal intelligence**
• **Intrapersonal intelligence**

Figure 2.6 Format for recording a child's strengths

> Abilities are often fluid rather than fixed: the degree to which someone succeeds at a challenge can be greatly influenced by factors such as time and place, the individual's mental state, the personal significance of the task, and the manner in which the problem is displayed. (Howe 1998)

I have often been asked about my views on using test results for identifying gifted children in the infant school. My answer has always been that while any source of information is useful, many factors may affect a child's performance in a test situation. One of them is that some very bright divergent thinkers may not respond well to closed questions and offer answers or explanations which are totally different to what is expected of them. Some general factors which present difficulties with identification of giftedness discussed in the next section also apply to tests.

Identifying underachieving gifted children

Knowing children's strengths and special talents helps the teacher to provide appropriate educational provision for them. However, the identification of talent is not always straightforward. Although most teachers can produce a list of their most able pupils if they are asked, they also acknowledge the complexity of the identification process and the difficulty in identifying pupils' potential abilities. Referring to children who fail to demonstrate their full potential in the classroom, HMI (1992) has this to say:

> Many teachers were aware of this problem and were able to point out pupils which in their judgement were underachieving for a variety of reasons, such as poor motivation, underdeveloped writing skills or physical problems.

Again, it is worth reiterating the fact that while many able pupils demonstrate their potential ability and produce high-quality work, there are others who fail to achieve their potential due to lack of self-esteem, or to a desire to mask their ability to avoid being different or to avoid being given 'extra' work which can often be repetitive and unstimulating. HMI's list (1992) of the factors which inhibit the progress of able pupils – low expectations of parents and teachers, a low level of self-esteem and a lack of support at home creating difficulties with study – can also contribute to difficulties with identification. In these particular cases teachers need to be extra vigilant and use close observation techniques to identify pupils' strengths.

The following indicators may be characteristic of underachieving able children. These are based on the list which Freeman (1998) has constructed from research evidence. Signs to look out for of underachievement of gifted pupils include the following:

- boredom and restlessness
- fluent orally, but poor written work
- hostility towards authority
- not knowing how to learn academically

- aspirations being too low for aptitudes
- poor test results, but asking creative questions
- work deteriorating over time.

I would like to bring this chapter to an end by sharing a case study with the readers. When asked to produce a list of gifted and talented children in her class, Joanne, a Year 1 teacher, was reluctant to do so. In the inner-city school where Joanne teaches, a large percentage of children do not speak English. Many of the families came from relatively deprived areas where children had to take care of themselves for much of the time. She explained her reasons by telling me about a girl in her class called Nisha. When Nisha started in her class on her arrival in England, Joanne felt there was something special about her, but was unable to make an assessment of her ability as she spoke no English. Joanne noticed that Nisha was 'very good' at some activities such as doing jigsaw puzzles and making patterns with beads. She spent much of her free time looking at puzzle books and attempting the ones which did not require reading. Most of the time she got them right. Nisha was given a generous amount of time by a support teacher who also enlisted the help of an interpreter who spoke Nisha's language. As she started picking up speaking and reading English, her progress was rapid in all areas. Within a year, Nisha could be listed as the 'best' in the class, as her teacher put it.

Summary

In this chapter aspects of identification of young gifted children were explored. The inherent challenge of defining giftedness was highlighted. Different perspectives on the nature of ability were introduced, inviting readers to construct their own framework in making judgements about children's abilities. Concerns and dilemmas felt by practitioners with regard to creating a list of gifted children while they are young were discussed. A way forward which does not involve labelling children as gifted and not gifted but making assessments of their special interests and strengths was proposed. A number of strategies for making effective identification of children's abilities were discussed and some models for observing children were suggested. The importance of the partnership between parents and teachers in the identification process was highlighted. Inherent difficulties in any form of assessment of children were discussed, with particular attention given to the identification of the underachieving gifted child.

3 Extending learning opportunities in the classroom

Aspects of identification of gifted children were dealt with in Chapter 2, where I highlighted the important principle that 'provision and identification' is a two-way process emphasising the word 'opportunities' in that context. If children are not provided with opportunities to demonstrate their special abilities, how can an adult make a true and accurate judgement of their capabilities? In this two-way process of identification and provision, the teacher's role is crucial. There is a need to rethink whether the view of education held by many, which is based on moving children on when they have mastered what is taught, is the most appropriate way of planning educational opportunities for gifted children. Many of us are familiar with Piaget's theory of learning which emphasises stages of learning and the concept of readiness before new educational experiences are introduced. Vygotsky, another innovative psychologist, put forward a different view that education precedes development and helps the child to move to the next stage. In his view all learning takes place within the child's Zone of Proximal Development (ZPD). Vygotsky (1978) maintains:

> the zone of proximal development ... is the distance between the developmental level as determined by independent problem solving and the level of potential development as determined through problem solving under adult guidance or in collaboration with more capable peers.

According to Vygotsky's principle, the role of education is to provide children with experiences within their ZPD by giving them suitably challenging tasks which they can tackle successfully with adult guidance.

The concept of challenge

What do we mean by challenging activities? I have often discussed the word 'challenge' with both practising teachers and teacher trainees and asked them to explain what they meant by 'offering challenge' within the curriculum. Many respond by interpreting the word 'challenge' to mean something that children did not 'already know' or a task which is 'difficult' to solve. This usually leads to a discussion of the concept of challenge by referring to examples in adult contexts. One of the examples I use, in the context of my own personal learning to illustrate a point, is as follows. Suppose I am presented with a task to find out how a telephone company works. This task is challenging if we use the definition that I do not 'already know' how it works and it is also a 'difficult' one for me. Under pressure or fear of punishment, I will carry out the project, but I am unlikely to make the most of it, for two reasons. First, I am not very interested in finding out how a telephone company works. Second, I would not be able to relate to a task asking me to 'find out all' I can without a context, as I would see it as a chore. In contrast, if the project requires me to find out all I can about porcelain dolls I may do a better job of this challenge because I am interested in the topic and have been collecting them since I was five years old. Even the challenge of 'find out all I can' will not deter me from making the best effort because of my personal passion for the topic. Even the first project – how a telephone company works – may have appealed to me more had it been presented within a meaningful context such as: *Imagine you are setting up a telephone company of your own; create a business plan and a proposal for a financial advance from the bank.*

During these discussions, the course participants and I try to explore some of the elements which would encourage children to take on challenging work with motivation and do their best. The following list is the outcome of one such discussion. When presenting younger children with 'challenging' work, it is useful to remember to include activities which:

- Relate to children's own interests. These are likely to increase their motivation and encourage them to make their best efforts. Any research carried out through reading, discussions with others or through the worldwide web would be more purposeful and focused.
- Offer a meaningful context for the work, again resulting in an increase in motivation and a more effective analysis of the demands of the task.
- Are placed just above the child's capability to tackle the task and fulfil the requirements. While a task which makes cognitive demands at an unrealistically high level may lead children to give up easily, tasks which require little effort will often be seen as pointless, and lead to boredom and frustration.

Offering children tasks with an appropriate level of challenge is itself a challenge. It is a complex process, but one which gets easier with experience. Many of the practical suggestions and examples provided in this and subsequent chapters should also help to achieve this goal.

An analysis of the special needs of young gifted children

In order to make a start in thinking about adequate provision for gifted youngsters let us make an analysis of their special needs. Although each gifted child is a special individual, a consideration of the cases of a sample of higher ability children should give us some insights into their particular needs. To place this within the framework of identification of gifted children that I have suggested in Chapter 2 there are two strands to consider: (1) viewing general ability as a continuum (Figure 1.1), and (2) viewing general ability within a Multiple Intelligences theory (described in Chapter 2). This may lead us to to think about the needs of gifted children in the following categories:

- The gifted child who learns fast and is advanced in several areas.
- The gifted child in 'domain-specific' or subject areas (e.g. mathematics).

The needs of the children in both categories should be recognised and provided for, although the way we go about it may be different. We should also adopt some general principles for whole-class provision.

One of the main objectives of teaching is to make appropriate educational provision to help all children to achieve their full potential; in the case of gifted children that aim is no different. We need to create a classroom environment which encourages children to become effective thinkers, problem-solvers and to exercise their creative and productive thinking capabilities. How do we make this happen? How do we make sure that a five-year-old who can read and write at the level of an eight-year-old is not bored in literacy lessons? What do we do with a group of seven -year-olds who are able to understand advanced concepts in mathematics and pursue sophisticated enquiries? Giving such children extra activities which they can easily manage is certainly not the solution. Letting them wait until the others catch up is not a sensible option. Experience suggests that a child, whose intellectual and personal interests and aptitudes are not met, can become easily bored, disruptive and start disliking school. Some children could also develop the view that schools do not provide what is relevant to their needs.

Before considering effective provision for gifted young children, think for a few minutes. Imagine yourself to be a child who is a fast learner and knows most of what is being taught to the class – during the literacy and numeracy lessons – or is learning other topics. Go through the day's teaching programme and ask yourself what that child's experience may be like. This should provide a useful background to start thinking about the needs of very able children and for considering practical provision.

Below, I will attempt to construct a list of what I consider to be the needs of gifted children. Their academic needs are considered in this chapter and in Chapters 4 and 5; their particular social and emotional needs are addressed in Chapter 6. The following list is based on two aspects: (1) an analysis of the list of learning attributes of gifted children, and (2) my own personal experience of working with them. Gifted children need to:

- have their special talents acknowledged and encouraged;
- be intellectually challenged;
- be able to exercise their curiosity, imagination and creativity;
- have opportunities to develop their particular interests;
- be able to work within a flexible organisation;
- work in a classroom environment which invites them to participate;
- be involved in their learning using a suitable and personal learning style;
- be able to reflect on their learning and improve the quality of their work.

At this point you may want to stop for a moment and look at your class list and the timetable, and make a note of whether and how efforts are being made in order to meet the above needs of your gifted children. Further, think about what evidence a visitor or an inspection team will see that you are meeting the needs of your brightest children.

Having considered some of the special needs of gifted young children, let us now think of how these may be implemented at classroom level. In the following sections I will explore some practical strategies that we can all employ in our classroom. Each section will provide some guiding principles and practical examples of how these principles can be translated into actual practice. Examples of subject-specific provision are given in Chapter 5. Before I present some general strategies for extending learning for gifted pupils, I must emphasise, however, that what I am proposing is essentially *good practice* for teaching all children although, within the context of this book, my discussions will refer to very able pupils, either as assessed through their performance or potential.

The sections are as follows:

- Providing a suitable classroom environment;
- Asking good-quality questions;
- Introducing higher levels of thinking into the curriculum;
- Encouraging creativity.

Providing a suitable classroom environment

During a recent in-service session a group of infant and nursery teachers reflected on what a rich classroom environment for the gifted would look like. One of the conclusions they came to was that it would be appropriate to have a lively environment for all children to participate in activities that interest them. Although the lessons in an infant classroom may have a more apparent structure and time constraints than in nursery classrooms we concluded that all classrooms should be vibrant, with excited learners who would be provided with opportunities to acquire new knowledge and skills. They would also be given opportunities for free explorations. Children would be encouraged to pursue their special interests and aptitudes – their own 'intelligences' if we were to refer to Gardner's Multiple Intelligences theory.

What does this mean in practice? There would be specific teaching sessions which target new learning by setting up experiences which are structured sufficiently to enable children to learn new ideas – facts such as the names of objects, colours, spellings, number names and the order in which numbers appear on a number line. Some questions would be phrased in such a way that children are encouraged to explore new ideas and experiment with concepts which are partly formed or understood. I have been impressed with classrooms where teachers have strived to achieve this balance – providing a structured learning programme as well as opportunities for free play and exploration. Structured learning opportunities provide children with a sound knowledge base on which to build and the opportunities to experiment to satisfy their innate curiosity. A classroom which provides this kind of environment should help us to both identify children's strengths and make provision for the fulfilment of their potential.

I will attempt to provide some examples of good practice, as I perceive it, of teachers making their classrooms a place which invites children to participate actively, explore ideas and be creative.

Displays

The classroom would be inviting, with lively and colourful wall and table displays. Displays would be labelled clearly; some would serve the purpose of reinforcing what has been taught, but others would pose questions or be invitations to take part in solving a problem or creating something new. Interactive displays have an important role to play. I am often surprised at the level of interaction generated by well-organised interactive displays. The following examples of tasks led to a high level of involvement of children, not only in the classroom but also by taking the ideas home to think about them and involving their families to bring back contributions for the display.

A 'Words within words' project

As described elsewhere (Koshy and Casey 1997a), this activity generated a great deal of enthusiasm and learning in classrooms. Some infant children were shown that there were words within words and then asked to think about words within other words. They were also asked to consider whether the words within words bore any relation to the meaning to the original word. For example, WHEEL has EEL within it, though EEL is not related to Wheel in its meaning. Similarly, BULLET has a BULL in it, though the bull does not influence the meaning of the the word BULLET. Children were also fascinated by 'small' animals found in 'bigger' animals – ANT within ELEPHANT – and larger animals found within words for smaller animals – CAT within CATERPILLAR. This ongoing activity leads children to a quest for words, resulting in their acquiring an increase in vocabulary, a greater awareness of the correct spellings of words and a sense of fascination for finding newer words. They also enjoyed the experience as the context appealed to them. A great deal of conversation in and out of the classroom focused on the nature of words. This activity appealed to all the children in the class, but children who had a special aptitude or interest in words produced impressive posters with extensive lists of words within words.

A problem-solving corner – Design a zoo

As part of a project on animals, in a Year 2 classroom, a group problem-solving activity – design a zoo – provided open-ended possibilities for children to be engaged in. After an initial introduction from the teacher, the challenge was set. Information on the preferences of the animals for their habitat and other instructions were provided. A corner in the classroom was especially prepared for displaying the contributions from each group of children. Children were told that they could provide their ideas in writing, pictures or models or as combinations, and they would be asked to share their ideas with an audience after a fortnight.

This activity also generated a great deal of discussion, involvement and some purposeful research. Children approached all the adults who showed willingness – classroom assistants, parents, dinner helpers and visitors – and all were drawn into the discussions of animals and their possible special needs when kept in a zoo. By the time of the presentation and sharing of everyone's ideas, which was the highlight of the week, there was strong evidence that most children had not only learned more animal names but had also acquired a greater understanding of the lives of animals and their surroundings.

A puzzle for the week

Organising a 'puzzle for the week' as an interactive display also allowed children opportunities to extend their thinking and refine strategies during a whole week of putting up solutions on the display board and the methods of how they solved the puzzle. The puzzle given in Figure 3.1 from the book of mathematical challenges (DfES 2000b) offered many opportunities for mathematical thinking and reasoning. Sometimes conversations, even in the playground, concentrated on the challenge offered by the puzzle.

Interest centres and targeted activities

Let us remind ourselves of the key word used throughout this book: **opportunity**. We need to create opportunities for children to respond to. This will enhance both identification and provision. Creating interest centres will provide an excellent opportunity for fulfilment of children's curiosity and interests. As research reported in Chapter 2 suggests, stimulating experiences provided in the first years of schooling enhance later achievement and foster positive attitudes. Well-organised interest centres should invite children to engage in activities, pursue their interests and show their individual strengths. These centres could be used for both independent and teacher directed activities. In nursery and reception classrooms the centres would provide areas where imaginative play and creative activities could take place. Both free play and structured sessions have their roles. Teachers could also direct both individuals and groups of children to these centres. In suggesting what might be included in the interest centres, I have incorprated information from two sources. First, as I have used Gardner's Multiple Intelligences theory as a basis for assessing children's individual strengths, it makes sense to take note of the seven intelligences suggested in his original framework for undersatnding issues relating to intelligence. Second, consideration needs to be given to the national framework for literacy and numeracy within which teachers in Key Stage 1 organise their teaching.

The ideas included here are by no means exhaustive; they are only examples. It is hoped that teachers will add to these and also make use of the expertise of the subject coordinators in their schools. In addition to the resources and materials, it would also

Figure 3.1 Snakes and ladders

be useful to have a display of current themes being taught, as well as themes of topical interest.

Apart from the usual resources – paper, pencils, felt-tip pens, crayons, scissors, glue, string and so on – the following includes a list of some materials which would provide opportunities for challenge and stimulation.

Creating a mathematics interest centre

Activities offered within this centre would encourage logical thinking and reasoning. They would create opportunities for exploring new ideas as well as testing out existing ideas. Activities would include all aspects of mathematics – number, data handling, measuring, pattern and shape and space. Ideally, invitations to participate, challenges and prompts would be displayed. Although Gardner has listed spatial awareness as separate from logical-mathematical intelligence, I have included this within the mathematics interest centre. Possible items include:

- roamers
- Lego
- cuisinnaire rods
- mathematical games
- resources for creating games and puzzles
- puzzles with a range of complexity
- squared paper
- pegboards
- dice
- mathematics journals
- number lines, including blank number lines
- number cards
- calculators
- challenging questions for exploration
- construction bricks
- computer software
- logiblocks
- biographies and posters of famous mathematicians
- CD-ROMs which have simulations of mathematical ideas such as angles, place value and so on
- books which illustrate mathematical ideas – counting, multiplication tables
- tangrams and mazes
- mathematics big books.

Setting up a language interest centre

The aim of the activities offered in this interest centre would be designed to instil an interest in words and developing language skills. There would be opportunities for creative writing and experimenting with words. Reading for pleasure will be an important activity within this centre. Possible items for this centre would include:

- a range of books – picture books, big books, factual books and reading books with different levels of complexity and reflecting current authors
- story-writing materials
- blank tapes and tape-recorders
- word searches and crosswords
- displays and tape-recordings of simple words and greetings from other languages – including tape-recorded ones from other children who speak the language
- computer software of writing packages
- word games and challenges
- magazines

- dictionaries
- biographies of well-known authors
- computers.

Organising a science centre

Within the framework of the Multiple Intellegences theory the following would be appropriate:

- books with a science focus
- beakers
- weather charts
- soil
- seeds
- pets
- fish tanks
- food labels
- textile samples
- shells
- biographies of well-known scientists and their discoveries
- cylinders, balances, weights, tapes
- telescope
- microscope
- objects for viewing
- computer simulations and films
- magnets
- mirrors
- thermometers
- iron filings, paper-clips
- instructions for growing crystals
- pictures and models of planets
- filmstrips, e.g. space.

Centre for artistic development

The materials and suggested activities within this centre would be designed to encourage artistic talents and to identify special aptitudes shown by children. Opportunities for drawing, painting, making pictures and collages, and playing mental imagery games would be provided. Materials within this centre would include:

- drawing materials
- colouring pens, charcoal
- plasticine, clay
- paint, paintbrushes and easels
- works of well-known artists
- cameras and film
- posters

- books showing the work of well-known artists and biographies
- Lego and bricks
- patterns, mosaics, sticky paper.

Organising for physical activities

Music and movement are part of all infant classroom activities. Some happen outside the classroom and others are organised in the classroom. Special talents in this area – what Gardner calls 'bodily kinaesthetic intelligence' – manifest in many forms. For example, it may be displayed during a drama session, a dance session or during PE. Physical dexterity and the imaginative use of materials can also be observed during building a structure or a model, or building a tent as part of a problem-solving activity. There are many opportunities in the day when a teacher may notice children's special talents in this particular area and acknowledge and encourage them to develop that interest further. In addition to the PE and Games equipment, most nursery and infant classrooms have the following equipment available:

- large and small blocks
- boxes
- puppets, dolls
- roamers
- hats, masks
- furniture
- woodwork tools
- wooden puzzles.

In addition to these you may set up three-dimensional displays of themes: either themes of current study or themes that catch the attention of children. Scenarios of shops, hospitals, restaurants, home corners and the seaside provide opportunities for demonstrating and enhancing their children's body skills.

Developing interpersonal intelligence

During a lecture on assessment my students and I surveyed the 'Appointments' sections of various newspapers. The specifications and criteria for applicants in most advertisements included 'interpersonal skills'. We discussed where in the school curriculum and organisation we included the development of interpersonal skills. Do we provide opportunities for children who show this talent or potential to be effective leaders? What kinds of activity encourage children to take on leadership roles and show their special talent in their people skills? Do we provide opportunities for children to be engaged in:

- group problem-solving
- leading discussions and debates
- organising presentations and displays
- taking on the role of representing a group

- planning a project
- organising speeches
- brainstorming exercises.

Establishing rules and discussions for group work and the development of listening skills would be part of training children to develop interpersonal skills as well as giving opportunities for demonstrating their interpersonal intelligence.

Developing intrapersonal skills

Knowing oneself well and being able to reflect on one's strengths is a talent worth developing. Some children may exhibit this from an early age; it is a desirable skill to develop in all children. If a child shows independence or prefers to work alone this may be only an indication of a disposition, not because of antisocial behaviour. The ability to reflect on one's strengths and weaknesses is often referred to as 'metacognition'. This aspect is described in more detail later in the book.

In the classroom some specific activities create the right kind of environment for this to happen. They are:

- encouraging children to keep personal journals; in the case of young children this may be in the form of pictures or tape-recordings
- working in a quiet area
- the opportunity to work on special projects and exhibit products with an attatched commentary.

I have often been asked how interest centres can operate in infant classrooms due to the pressures of the curriculum. In a nursery classroom, setting up these activity centres and specially designed programmes seems easier to manage, but in practice many infant teachers have set up interest centres in their classrooms very effectively. They see these areas being designated for access at 'choice' times or for directing children who may show particular interest in an area.

The role of play

One of the ways of providing a rich environment in classrooms is through play. Play helps children to learn features of their environment through exploration. By experimentation they learn to predict what may happen following their initiatives. Given opportunities, children would show their interests and special aptitudes during play. David (1999) maintains that although there is much debate about what exactly play means to practitioners, there is strong evidence that children's long-term achievements in school are promoted by early learning which is self-directed. She supports her view by providing research evidence of this (Sylva 1998) and by quoting Ofsted (1993), placing much emphasis on the balance between learning through self-directed play and learning through teacher-directed activities in classrooms for young children.

I have spent many joyful hours watching young children at play making up games with their own rules, constructing a house for an imaginary family or planning a party. The quality of their play certainly depends on what opportunities are provided for them. Observing them at play and reflecting on ways play can extend children's knowledge and thinking, I believe the following principles may provide a set of guidelines for assessing the quality of what is on offer. During play:

- Children should be given a range of opportunities which would encourage the different intelligences discussed in Chapter 2.
- Materials should be on offer where children can have access to them. The practice of an adult deciding which puzzle to put out on the table may restrict a child's natural interest and choice.
- Ask questions which encourages children to move forward in their thinking.
- Adult scaffolding is necessary for encouraging children to demonstrate their ability and potential.
- There should be a balance of free imaginative play and structured activities. Free play encourages problem-solving and creativity whereas structured activities will help children in their language development and concept formation.
- Children have the chance to show their Zone of Proximal Development (ZPD), as Vygotski (1978) describes it.

Providing a rich classroom environment is the first step towards both effective identification and provision for gifted young children. It is unlikely that young children will show their talents in an environment which does not provide a fertile soil for growth and one which makes no cognitive demands.

Asking good-quality questions

Curiosity is a basis for learning. This is true for all age groups and in the case of younger children the level of curiosity if often very high. Most checklists which describe gifted children list curiosity as one of the attributes exhibited by them. Wanting to find out about things, exploring new perspectives and pathways, making conjectures and testing them are features of effective learning experiences, and it is through questioning that an adult can guide children to follow paths of worthwhile enquiry. The introduction of the National Numeracy and Literacy Strategies has enhanced teachers' questioning skills at Key Stage 1, but much more needs to be done. I consider it one of the most important aspects to consider within a book which focuses on gifted young children.

Is there a theoretical rationale for attributing an important role to questioning skills in the learning process? In a behaviourist mode of learning, questions would be asked to test what has been learned – often the responses are based on rote learning. No account may be taken of a range of abilities or of the cognitive processes involved in the learning. In contrast, if we were to subscribe to a constructivist philosophy of learning in which a child constructs his or her own learning, building up a network of knowledge, then asking probing questions would be an effective way of assessing the level of children's conceptual understanding. Further, within a social constructivist philosophy, which places an important emphasis on social interactions in the process of learning, the role of good questioning skills becomes really important. Teachers, based on the responses they receive from the children to their questions, can move on the children's thinking after ascertaining the quality of their conceptual understanding. Vygotsky's theory of Zone of Proximal Development, described earlier in this chapter, lends further support to the importance of asking the right kinds of question. By asking probing questions the adult is able to judge the level of a child's actual and potential development and be able to offer 'scaffolding' to assist his or her development.

The quality of the questions we ask makes a difference to the quality of the learning that takes place. Teachers always ask questions. These questions may have different purposes. There are questions which relate to management; these are necessary for the smooth organisation of the classroom. Then there are questions which invite responses from children on their learning – both testing new knowledge as well as questions which assess the level of cognitive function which leads to a robust understanding of concepts.

By asking the right kinds of questions important for all children, but especially in the case of gifted children who process information faster than their peers, teachers can extend their thinking. Asking the right types of questions will enable teachers to match learning objectives to the abilites of the child.

Let us now consider the two main types of questions – closed and open-ended questions. There is a place for both types in a classroom. Closed questions are often asked to test children's knowledge of facts. The responses are immediate and are often short. Open-ended questions can be phrased in such a way that more detailed information on the type of understanding of concepts may be assessed. These questions may lead to more questions both from the teacher and the learner. They may also create cognitive conflict, as Piaget describes it, in the learner, and resolving the conflicts can lead to better understanding and more effective application of concepts.

A few years ago, a group of infant and nursery teacher researchers who worked with our centre at the university carried out an audit of the kind of questions they asked the children. The following features emerged.

A substantial proportion of the questions which both children and the teachers asked were related to management and organisation. Examples were:

Teacher: Where do we keep our paper, Shane? Can you tell everyone?
Children: Is this all right, miss? Is this what you mean?

It was also noted that a significant number of the questions which were asked by the teacher started with ' What...', 'Which...' and so on. These elicited short responses. In an attempt to improve pupil responses, the teachers changed their style of the questions to types of question which started with *'Why...', 'How...','Where...'* and *'Can you tell me more about...?'*. The results were very heartening. The quality of the responses given by children was greatly enhanced. The examples given in Figures 3.2 and 3.3 were collected from young children either as tape-recordings or written down by their teachers.

Why is...?

Figure 3.2 What questions would you like to ask?

Would you rather ...?

Bird or butterfly?
'I would rather be a bird because I can fly away for a free holiday.
I don't want to be a butterfly because people collect butterflies and stick pins in them'

River or bridge?
'I would rather not be a bridge because people drive cars and buses over me.
In a river I would have lots of fish as my friends'

'I would rather be a pencil so I could write lots of stories. You can write stories anywhere'

Would you rather be...?

A chair or a carpet?
A bat or a ball?
A river or a bridge?
A child or a grown-up?
A pencil or a book?
A flower or a butterfly?
A bird or a butterfly?

'I want to be a magic carpet because I can fly and no one would hoover me'.

'I would rather be myself so I can enjoy butterflies, birds and flowers'

Child or grown-up?
'I would rather be a child because you get lots of presents.
You can hide in small places.
If you are old you can't get through little gaps.
You live longer if you are younger'

Ask the children:

Figure 3.3 'Would you rather' questions

The above examples speak for themselves. Teachers who took part in the project acknowledged that the responses provided by the children often surprised them and were good indicators of their ability to think and reason.

How do good questioning skills assist in the process of learning? Consider the following statements within the context of your own teaching:

- The why and how types of question help to extend children's thinking.
- Probing questions help to assess the level of a child's understanding and cognitive functioning.
- Questions asked of individual children help to identify children's special aptitudes.
- Information gathered by asking open-ended questions helps to extend children's thinking by suggesting extensions.
- Targeted questions help children to resolve misunderstandings and misconceptions .

Who asks the questions?

During a problem-solving activity, I once asked a group of six-year-old children to think of questions one could ask about tubes of *Smarties*. They found this process surprisingly difficult even after I initiated some questions. One child explained that in their class the teacher always asked the questions and the children answered them, not the other way round. After much persuasion they started posing questions, and it was only when I invited everyone to ask the most challenging question they could think of that I realised how capable they were of using their hypotheses and conjectures as a basis for their questions.

The process of asking questions enables children to think in more depth and analyse ideas. Questions posed by themselves are more likely to lead to more meaningful enquiries and more independent learning.

The ways in which teachers can provide challenging learning experiences by asking higher-order questions is discussed in the next section.

Introducing higher levels of thinking into the curriculum

As part of a study carried out at the university my colleagues and I designed a set of principles as a basis for designing good-quality activities for more able primary school children. The principles we adopted for designing the activities were that they:

- must be set in a motivating context
- must provide intellectual challenge
- have potential for differentiation with multi-level outcomes
- provide opportunities for both group and individual work
- provide opportunities for creative exploration
- enable children to evaluate and reflect on their work
- incorporate higher levels of thinking.

As we wrote and trailled the materials with a group of teachers, what emerged very strongly was that the principles we set were based on 'good practice' that all teachers must strive for and the activities were 'good for all children', as the teachers put it. As a result, the activities were used with all children rather than with just a selected group. Not surprisingly, the activities provided a means to identify talents and strengths in some children which had not been identified before. There are many frameworks one could use for designing challenging activities for children. The model I have chosen, Bloom's Taxonomy (1956), has been used by hundreds of teachers who have attended our in-service programmes; it is also used extensively in other countries such as Australia, New Zealand and the USA for the past few decades.

Bloom's Taxonomy of the cognitive domain introduces six levels of thinking. They are:

1 Knowledge
2 Comprehension
3 Application
4 Analysis
5 Synthesis
6 Evaluation

The first three – knowledge, comprehension and application – are often referred to as lower-order skills. They would involve learning basic facts, restating and applying them. Most gifted children process information faster than their peer groups and are more capable of being engaged in the higher levels – analysis, synthesis and application. Although the levels of thinking are classified into six levels and are demonstrated with specific examples, the intention is not to phrase questions or plan activities, rigidly targeting each level of the taxonomy. You will see that it is more sensible and practical to think in terms of designing activities which incorporate 'higher' levels of thinking. For the purpose of curriculum planning, it is useful to consider the higher levels of thinking making increased demands on the cognitive processes. In the following section, I will provide my interpretation and explanation of the six levels of the taxonomy. I Then will try to illustrate them by using examples to show how the six levels of the taxonomy can provide us with a solid framework for planning.

Knowledge

This level is about acquisition of facts and requires recall of facts. At this level we ask children to identify, list or recall information. Learning facts may involve some repetition for some children but the most able may already have a substantial amount of knowledge of facts. Learning facts is important as a solid knowledge base is necessary for carrying out further investigations. Names of animals, parts of the human body, number names and symbols and names of scientific equipment may be classified at this level.

Comprehension

At this level children are able to restate what they know and describe what they have learned. It does not involve much challenge. Paraphrasing what has been learned, answering questions based on a text or writing a summary of what has been read or told are examples of activities at this level. In the classroom, describing an animal, comprehension exercises, counting on using a number line or counting out six objects to match the symbol six are examples of work at this level.

Application

At this level children are asked to apply what they have learned in practical and simple problem-solving contexts. This does require a more demanding level of cognitive processing than the previous two. Matching an animal to a given description or solving a mathematical problem using addition or multiplication facts would require application.

Analysis

This is a more challenging level as it requires thinking in depth. At this level situations and ideas are broken down into component parts and studied in more detail. Categorising information and looking for patterns are features of activities at this level. Asking children to compare two recipes or focusing on the interconnected nature of mathematical operations, identifying mathematical patterns and analysing the structures of words are examples of such activities.

Synthesis

I often refer to this as the one which offers full scope for imagination and creativity. It involves a more complex level of thinking as one moves away from what has been taught and understood to create new ideas or design original products. The work produced at this level would be more original. By looking at ideas in a different way or asking the question *'What if...'* new ideas or products are created. Re-creating the script of a fairy-tale, designing a new toy or a designer animal are examples of working at the synthesis level.

Evaluation

This is the highest level of the taxonomy and one, in my experience, which children find quite challenging. It involves evaluating ideas, products and thought processes. I always suggest that evaluation and analysis are used concurrently, as evaluation involves analysis and making a judgement based on what has been found. Giving opinions and backing up the ideas with sensible arguments is a skill worth cultivating. Setting up criteria for evaluating your own and others' products, creating reflective diaries (verbal or in writing) and self-assessment are examples of activities at this level of the taxonomy.

I will now illustrate how the six levels of the taxonomy can form the basis of planning by giving two examples.

The first example, in Table 3.1, shows how the six levels of the taxonomy can form the basis of designing questions relating to a fairy-tale – *Goldilocks and the Three Bears.* Although they are presented in the form of questions, they may be easily designed as activities.

Table 3.1 The story of *Goldilocks and the Three Bears* – an example of how Bloom's Taxonomy can be used in planning

Levels	Examples of questions/activities
Knowledge	Can you make a list of the characters in the story? Where did the three bears live? What did Goldilocks eat at the Bears' home? Make a poster showing the number of chairs and beds in the bears' house. What was the colour of Goldilocks' hair?
Comprehension	Can you tell the story in your own words? What happened to baby bear's chair? Draw a picture to show what happened in the story. Why did Goldilocks like baby bear's porridge and his bed the best? If Goldilocks had dark hair what would you call her?
Application	Find the characters in the story in a wordsearch. What would have happened if Goldilocks came to your house? Find another bear story, read it and tell us that story. Make up a conversation about what happened in the house when the bears returned home. Make a model of the three bears' house. Find out what you can about bears' hibernation.
Analysis	Which part of the story did you like best? How are bears different from other pets which people keep? Why do we have teddy bears? Can you think of some reasons why everyone must have a toy bear? Ask ten people in the class how many toy bears they have at home. Make up a display to show this. Find out what one kind of food bears eat and think up a recipe for making a nice dish for them.

Synthesis	Can you think of a different ending to the story? Write a letter to Goldilocks pretending you are the baby bear. Invent a new bear character and write some sentences to tell about an adventure she or he might have. Tape-record your story and, using the glove puppet, tell the story to others at story time. You have been hired to design a new home for the three bears using materials you like.
Evaluation	What did you think of the story? Daddy bear was caught by bad people who used him to do tricks in the street during the day and chained him up all night. Write a letter to a newspaper to show how unfair this is and how the rest of the family feels. Write the story of the three bears as if it happened in the present. What kind of an animal would you like to visit you? By magic it has learned to talk.

Table 3.2 Example of a topic on weather to illustrate the increasing levels of thinking demands within the six levels

Topic – Weather

Knowledge

- What do you know about weather?
- Make up a list of words you use to talk about weather.
- Draw a picture to show the different weather words.
- What is today's weather like?

Comprehension

- Describe what rain looks like.
- What is the difference between snow and rain?
- What kind of clothes do you wear when it is hot? Where can you find a weather forecast?
- Cut out the weather forecast for every day of the week and check whether it is correct.

Application

- Can you make a weather chart?
- Can you make a list of what we do in different weather conditions?
- Can you match the weather to the word clues?
- Make up a wordsearch to find weather words.
- Write a weather report.

Analysis
- Which weather do you like best? Hot? Sunny? Rainy? Say why.
- Would you rather be a raindrop or a snowflake?
- If you had a chance to talk to someone from a weather station, what five questions would you ask?

Synthesis
- If you could choose the weather or season which would you choose? Why?
- What would happen if it never rains?
- Pretend you are a raindrop. Write a story about yourself.
- Design an item of clothing which can be used in all weather conditions.

Evaluation
- What is the most interesting thing you have learned about weather?
- Think of one thing about weather you would like to find out a little more about.
- What is your favourite weather? How would you feel if that weather stayed all the time?

The two examples given in Tables 3.1 and 3.2 should offer a possible framework for differentiating the tasks and should be applicable in any curriculum areas. I have included a possible framework for using Bloom's Taxonomy to plan mathematical activities in my book *Teaching Mathematics to Able Children* (Koshy 2001).

Encouraging creativity

When I visit nursery classrooms I often see children playing with various equipment and assuming various roles with ebullient curiosity. Their potential imagination and creativity seem boundless, yet sadly external constraints of subsequent years seem to impose forms of repression on this mental vitality. The fun and the pleasure of fantasy and imagination somehow seem to disappear from the classroom as children grow up. Is the process of education a training for conformity within an adult world requiring task performance in clearly defined, deterministic goals? The sad consequence of this possible decrease in opportunities for creative thinking and productivity may result in the fact that many adults may never have the opportunity to experience the enjoyment and satisfaction of creating something. This is reflected in one of my favourite quotations on creativity that I often use in my lectures:

> Many people seem to possess seeds of creativeness, but the environment fails to provide the proper nourishment for growth. Therefore these people never fully live.
>
> (Parnes 1982: 352)

What do we mean by creativity? It has many different definitions and interpretations. By creativity in the classroom, I mean letting children 'look at things differently' without rigidly stressing convergent predetermined answers all the time.

It is about letting children fly, considering a range of options and possibilities. In my experience – confirmed by the comments from many practising teachers – once you let children explore and follow their own thoughts and directions, the products are often of a superior quality. Besides, children start enjoying school work when they are given some freedom for enquiry.

Where do we start? In the previous section when I introduced Bloom's taxonomy, I referred to the 'synthesis' level as the 'creative' level when new directions are taken and new products considered. All the activities suggested within this level will encourage creative thinking. In the following section, I will describe some further examples of the types of activity that can be offered to younger children and which are designed to promote creativity. These sessions do not have to lead to tangible written outcomes. Discussions, debates or the production of leaflets should be perfectly acceptable. How many times have we heard children complaining about having to write stories, whereas many of them may construct better stories if the choice of not writing them down is given?

How would your children respond to the following ideas?

- Imagine what would happen if what is usually taken for granted did not occur. What would happen if:
  - all the rulers/clocks disappeared
  - one day the sun did not rise
  - all the cars disappeared.
- Design a logo representing what the school has to offer.
- Write an advertisement to sell something that you are not keen on yourself. What encouraging words can you use? Figure 3.4 gives two examples of advertisements from children from Highview Primary school, Battersea, London.
- Can you write a story for a given headline in the local Newspaper (e.g. *Local hero saves a badger*)?
- Instead of asking children to complete a story ask them to write a few paragraphs about what happened before the start of the story.
- Look at another point of view. For example, you are a squirrel for a day: write about your experiences (Figure 3.5). This provides opportunities for showing both inter- and intrapersonal intelligences – being able to think about oneself and feel empathy. Rewrite the story of Little Red Riding Hood from the wolf's point of view, arguing that he is not a bad person after all (Figure 3.6)!

Summary

In this chapter aspects of classroom provision were considered. The role of the adult in the process of identifying children's potential ability and interests was emphasised. The concept of challenge was analysed in the context of what is offered in the classroom. Four aspects of effective classroom provision were considered. The importance of providing a rich environment and the role of purposeful and intellectually challenging questions were discussed. A framework for curriculum planning incorporating higher levels of thinking and opportunties for creative productivity was also offered.

Please
plese eat the Cabige it makes you stog like sweets. and it is helthey. It tastes
cabbage ... strong ... healthy
It makes you grwe big in no time. It is makes you butigle.
grow ... beautiful

age. 6.

If you eat salad it will make you healfy and big and strong. Salad tastes like sweets. Salad is delishous.
delicious

Figure 3.4 Two examples of children's advertisments

Year 2

morning

In the morning I got out of my feathery little Patch in the hollow

hidden

of a tree to have my brakfast that I had hiddin at the bottam

except

of the tree. But when I got there they weren't there exfet for a

corner

mini one crunched up in a coner. Never mind there was time to

find some more for lunch I thought. So off I went to the

Park to find some scrumshs nuts for lunch. As soon as

I had found them it was lunch already so soon I thought

So I ate my nut's. Then I had alittle sleep When I

awoke it was the morning agian to start another sqral day.

The End

Honeywell School Wandsworth

Figure 3.5 Squirrel for a day

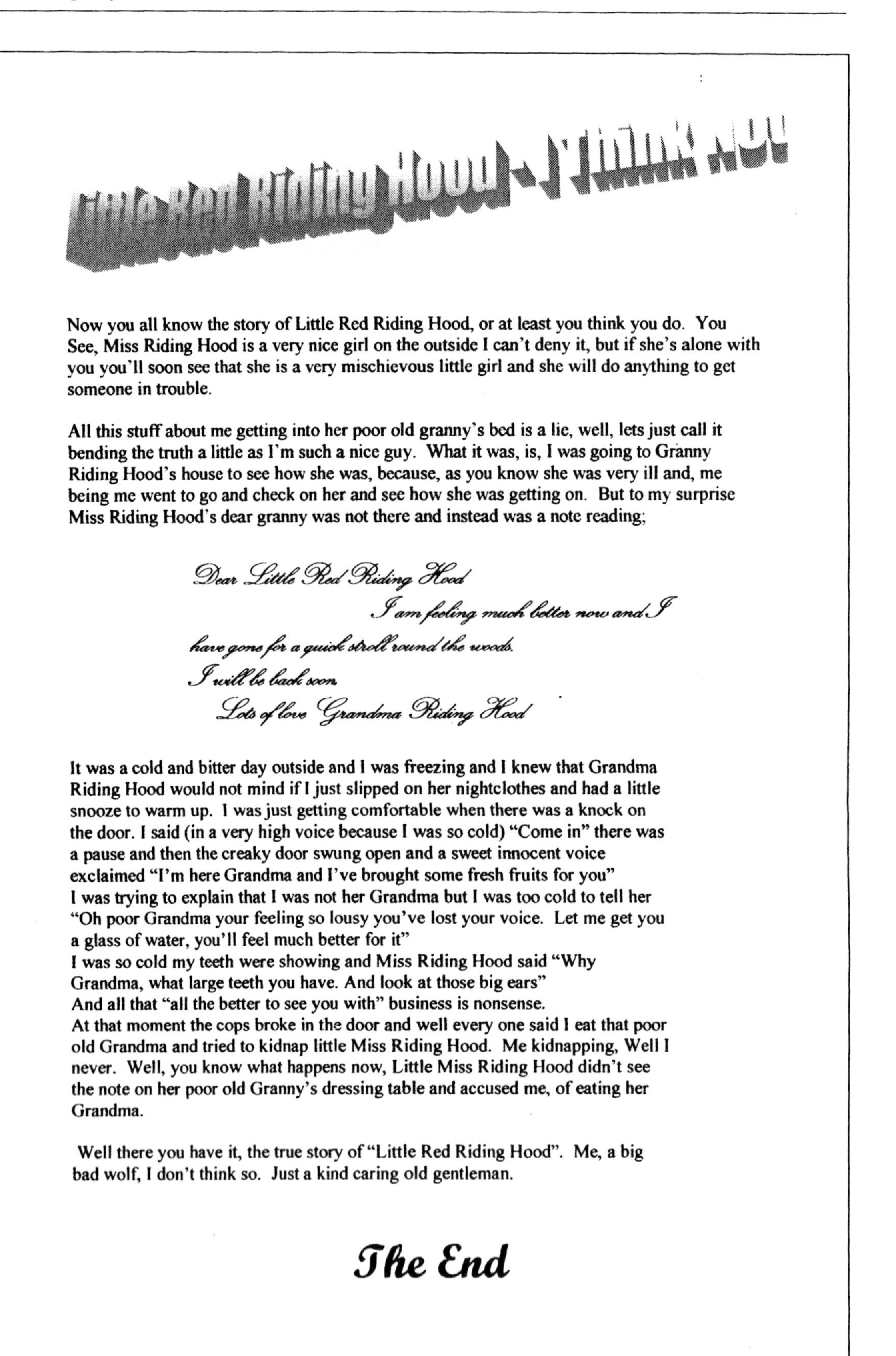

Little Red Riding Hood - I Think Not

Now you all know the story of Little Red Riding Hood, or at least you think you do. You See, Miss Riding Hood is a very nice girl on the outside I can't deny it, but if she's alone with you you'll soon see that she is a very mischievous little girl and she will do anything to get someone in trouble.

All this stuff about me getting into her poor old granny's bed is a lie, well, lets just call it bending the truth a little as I'm such a nice guy. What it was, is, I was going to Granny Riding Hood's house to see how she was, because, as you know she was very ill and, me being me went to go and check on her and see how she was getting on. But to my surprise Miss Riding Hood's dear granny was not there and instead was a note reading;

Dear Little Red Riding Hood
I am feeling much better now and I have gone for a quick stroll round the woods.
I will be back soon.
Lots of love Grandma Riding Hood

It was a cold and bitter day outside and I was freezing and I knew that Grandma Riding Hood would not mind if I just slipped on her nightclothes and had a little snooze to warm up. I was just getting comfortable when there was a knock on the door. I said (in a very high voice because I was so cold) "Come in" there was a pause and then the creaky door swung open and a sweet innocent voice exclaimed "I'm here Grandma and I've brought some fresh fruits for you"
I was trying to explain that I was not her Grandma but I was too cold to tell her "Oh poor Grandma your feeling so lousy you've lost your voice. Let me get you a glass of water, you'll feel much better for it"
I was so cold my teeth were showing and Miss Riding Hood said "Why Grandma, what large teeth you have. And look at those big ears"
And all that "all the better to see you with" business is nonsense.
At that moment the cops broke in the door and well every one said I eat that poor old Grandma and tried to kidnap little Miss Riding Hood. Me kidnapping, Well I never. Well, you know what happens now, Little Miss Riding Hood didn't see the note on her poor old Granny's dressing table and accused me, of eating her Grandma.

Well there you have it, the true story of "Little Red Riding Hood". Me, a big bad wolf, I don't think so. Just a kind caring old gentleman.

The End

Figure 3.6 Little Red Riding Hood

4 Organising children's learning

In Chapter 4 we considered general strategies for making effective provision for children in the classroom. Creating an inviting physical environment, the role of questioning, a framework for planning intellectually challenging activities and how to encourage creativity were discussed. In this chapter, I will explore strategies for organising children's learning and ways in which we can encourage children to be more effective learners. The aim of education is to provide maximum opportunities for learning and self-fulfilment for all children. In that context the principles set out by Renzulli (1994) for talent development are worthy of consideration. Renzulli proposes that:

- Each learner is unique, and therefore all learning opportunities must be examined in ways that take into account the abilities, interests, and learning style of the individual.
- Learning is more effective when students enjoy what they are doing, and therefore learning experiences must be constructed and assessed with as much concern for enjoyment as for other goals.
- Learning is more meaningful and enjoyable when content (i.e. knowledge) and process (thinking skills and modes of enquiry) are learned within the context of a real and present problem.
- Some formal instruction may be used for enrichment learning and teaching. A major goal of enrichment learning is to enhance knowledge and acquisition of skills gained through teacher instruction with applications of knowledge and skills that result from children's constructions of meaning.

Within the general principles set out above, I will present some strategies for organising learning for younger gifted children. Six themes introduced in this chapter have support both from international research and my own work with teachers of younger children and with groups of children. I believe that we can enhance learning opportunities for young gifted children by:

1 Modifying the curriculum to match children's learning needs.
2 Providing opportunities for children to follow their individual interests.
3 Taking note of children's individual learning styles.

4 Assessing children's individual strengths.
5 Involving adults in the child's learning process.
6 Considering organisational issues.

Modifying the curriculum to match children's learning needs

A recurrent theme which appears in national newspapers and in letters we receive at the able children's centre at Brunel University is about the frustration experienced by young gifted children who have previously mastered most of the teaching content being taught to the class. The case of a four-year-old, who was described as 'extremely bright' who can 'read fluently' and can tell you 'what an isthmus is and draw a parallelogram', was described in *The Daily Telegraph* (1996), and highlights the level of knowledge a young child may possess. Whether, as in many cases, the children have taught themselves the content or were taught at home, the result could be the same. The teacher has to keep these children stimulated and maintain their interest in learning. Giving them material which is too easy or giving them more of the same can lead to boredom. In such situations, children can develop negative feelings about their school and towards the process of learning. This is serious at any stage of a child's schooling, and particularly so in the first years of schooling when attitudes are formed and motivation is put into gear – anything but neutral, but preferably high! I know of such children who react either by going off school, becoming disruptive or hiding their high ability for fear of extra work which they can legitimately see as a punishment for being 'very good' at their work. The challenge for the teacher is to provide these children with worthwhile activities and to encourage them to employ their abundant curiosity and mental energy to good use.

How do we achieve this? There is certainly a need for modifying what is on offer. Here are some possible strategies a teacher could employ.

- Explore the possibility of using the facts and skills already acquired by the child in applications of that knowledge base for solving problems and situations requiring more sophisticated modes of thought. This could be done by giving children an activity which starts off with some complexity or by giving an activity which would provide opportunities for open-ended outcomes within each child's ability and disposition.
- Expose the child to a variety of cross-curricular contexts so as to generate a special interest, which could motivate that child to expand both the knowledge base and techniques of application.

Examples of the first strategy may be be seen in Figures 4.1 and 4.2. The first example, in Figure 4.1, is that of a group of very able Year 2 children being given an activity involving the idea of 'optimisation' during a mathematics session, when the rest of the children were practising 'working out change' from shopping bills which would have been too easy for the top group.

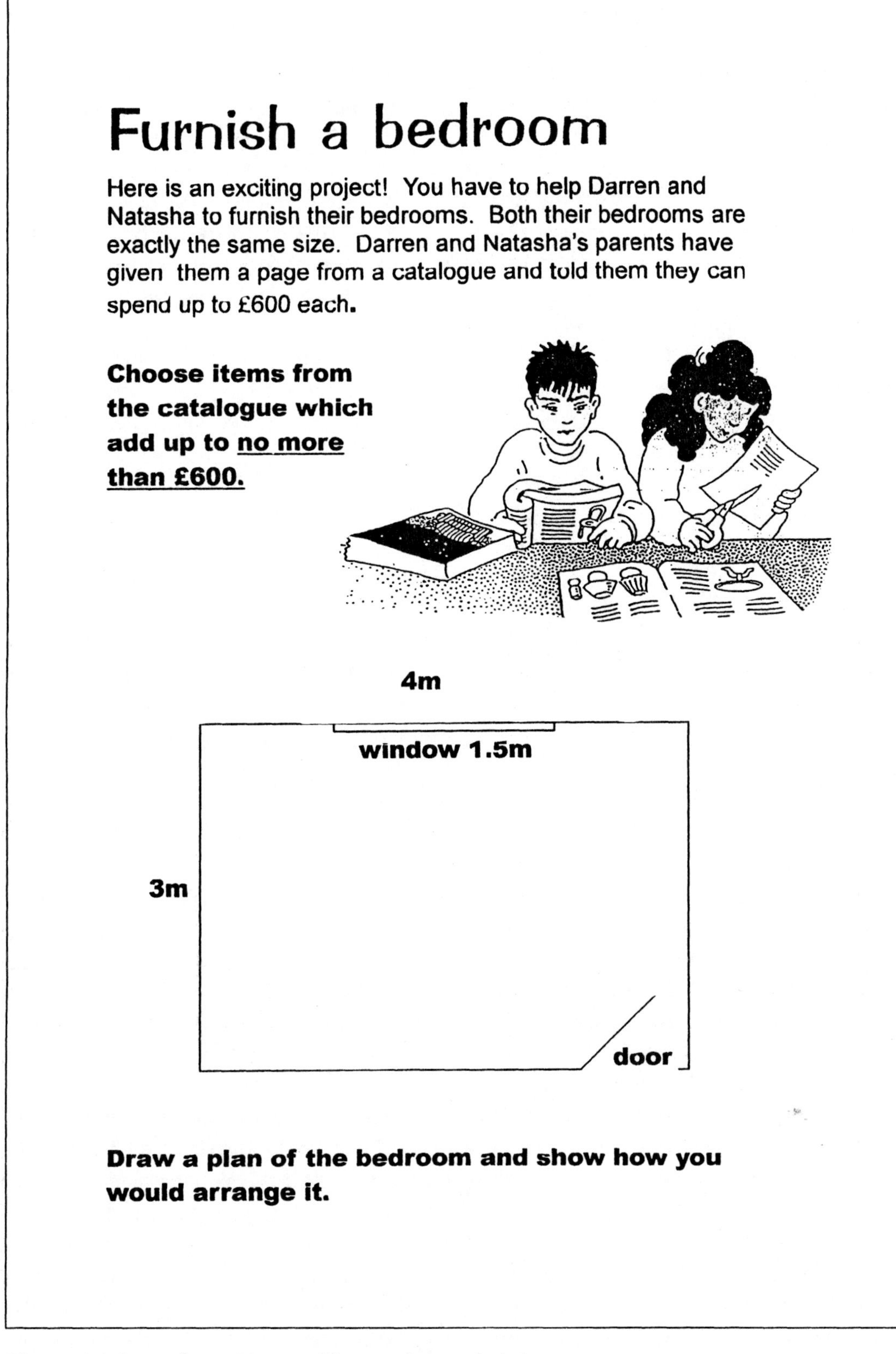

Furnish a bedroom

Here is an exciting project! You have to help Darren and Natasha to furnish their bedrooms. Both their bedrooms are exactly the same size. Darren and Natasha's parents have given them a page from a catalogue and told them they can spend up to £600 each.

Choose items from the catalogue which add up to no more than £600.

Draw a plan of the bedroom and show how you would arrange it.

Figure 4.1 A mathematics problem-solving activity

Giving them what everyone would be doing first followed by a problem-solving activity would have been seen by the children as unfair and a punishment for knowing more than the others. So the teachers gave them pages from a catalogue and asked them to help plan a bedroom. Some items had both simple discounts and percentage discounts and there were 'special offers' which involved complex calculations for comparing the best buys using the idea of proportion. Although discounts, percentages and ideas of ratio are not in the syllabus for this group of children they had no difficulty in finding out what they needed to know in order to apply these ideas. The motivating context did, of course, enhance the quality of their participation. The activity in Figure 4.2 was given to all the children in the same class as a substitute, as I suggested, for their routine work of finding words in the dictionary. While all the children enjoyed the challenge, some of the outstanding contributions came from the most able.

The other strategy to help children fulfil their learning potential is to enable them to pursue activities which appeal to their special interests. I have found this strategy to be very effective and discuss this in more detail in the next section. When I suggest that children are given opportunities to select a special topic for exploration, an understandable question that often arises is: Where does the time come from? This is where the idea of Curriculum Compacting (Renzulli 1994) proves to be a helpful strategy. The process of Curriculum Compacting is a strategy developed at the National Research Centre for the Gifted and Talented at the University of Connecticut and its director, Professor Joseph Renzulli, suggests that the time we save by compacting the curriculum – streamlining what is taught to children by cutting out parts which they already know – may be bought 'back' by the students to be spent in another way.

The process of Curriculum Compacting needs to be organised carefully. The starting point for this process is to accept that all children need to learn facts and skills, but a gifted child may do this at a faster rate. So first we need to ascertain that they have acquired basic facts and skills at an appropriate level. This can be done through questioning, individual interviews, assessing the contents of individual portfolios or from parents' feedback. Once the level of the child's knowledge is assessed, the teacher has to make decisions about what needs to be cut out from the taught part of the curriculum and also what to do with that time. It would be unwise to ask a child to use that time to practise legible writing or to tidy up the classroom. Suggesting that the child pursue a topic of personal interest is one effective way of using this 'saved' time. Getting children to pursue their 'passion' topic involves careful thought and planning as described later in this chapter.

When compacting the curriculum it is useful to remember that a child may not be proficient in all areas of the curriculum. Each child's case needs to be studied carefully against the suggested learning outcomes for the class and what is to be taught to the class during the week or term before cutting out parts of the child's learning experiences. The time saved by compacting parts of the curriculum need not be used exclusively for special personal projects. Enriching extensions to other work in the classroom may also be suggested. I have seen many examples of this such as writing a book, problem-solving, using programmable toys and organising a presentation or a production.

ENGLISH

Word treasure

Have you ever wondered where words actually came from?

Was the word 'chair' invented by someone?
What about 'air'? Did 'chair' come after 'air'?
Why should 'air' be in 'chair' as if it is a cushion?

It is not always possible to find answers to these types of questions, but you can have fun inventing meanings for words.

NOW

Your challenge is to produce a list of words and incorrect meanings (preferably funny), but with the correct meaning always shown and checked with the help of a dictionary.

Study the examples on the resource sheets.

Word Treasure

1. Outcast
   a. Out of the school assembly
   b. Someone rejected from his family.
   c. A make of caster sugar.
2. Maximum
   a. Max's mum
   b: Maxim birds that say 'um'
   c. The greatest amount.
3. Carnation
   a. The 'Car of the Nation award'.
   b. A flower with a sweet smell.
   c. A car that travels from one nation to another.
4. Candlestick
   a. A stick used as a candle.
   b. A clock in the shape of a candle.
   c. A holder for a candle.
5. Carrot
   a. A car that rots
   b. A car with 'rot' on the license plate.
   c. An orange vegetable.
6. Microwave.
   a. A little wave.
   b. A kind of cooker
   c. A small wave at the seaside.

Figure 4.2 A word challenge activity

Providing opportunities for children to follow their individual interests

The principles set out by Renzulli that learning is more effective if the learner enjoys what he or she is doing is the cornerstone of what is being proposed in this section. I have often thought about Dewey's assertion, in 1916, when I evaluate children's interest in a topic of exploration:

> To be interested is to be absorbed in, wrapped up in, carried away by, some object. To take an interest is to be on the alert, to care about, to be attentive. We say of an interested person that he has both lost himself in some affair and that he has found himself in it. Both terms express the engrossment of the self in the subject.

When you see a child sitting in a corner absorbed in an activity or a set of objects, seemingly not learning what is on the planned schedule, or a non-conformist child disregarding the instructions to follow a worksheet, it may be worth reminding ourselves of Dewey's words.

As mentioned above asking children to follow their special interest and undertake an in-depth study may seem easy, but the whole process needs careful preparation and organisation. The first challenge is to find out what a child's real passion is. Observing children during their 'free' choosing time or busy at the interest centres should give some indicators. Listening to their conversations and studying the entries in parents surveys could also provide useful pointers. In addition, asking the children to complete (with adult help if necessary) an 'interest sheet' may reveal a personal passion for a topic.

Are there other ways in which we can identify a child's special interests? The following may provide indicators. A child may:

- bring out the topic of interest, collection or hobby within a formal or informal discussion;
- spend time drawing or doodling about aspects of a specific topic;
- spend time reading or browsing through books on a special topic;
- ask questions about a specific topic;
- be seen at an interest area showing curiosity and exploring specific objects.

Melissa's project

Five-year-old Melissa is in the reception class. She is very advanced for her age in several areas of the curriculum. Her reading age is eight and she is a good factual writer. Although her handwriting is not well developed, she can word-process fluently and produce work of a very high standard. I am told that Melissa 'loves school' and is 'excited' about being there. She is allowed to spend some time in the reading corner. When I met her, she was involved in a special individual project on 'butterflies', and proudly showed me her folder which she called her 'Book of Butterflies'. Melissa's teacher, Stephanie, found out about her special interest in butterflies from her parent survey and a follow-up interview with her parents. She was very pleased with this discovery because:

> this was heaven sent. Within three hours of meeting Melissa, I knew I could have problems. She was a very fluent reader, she could recite numbers correctly up to a hundred and beyond, could spell many words and tell the time accurately. Working with other children in the class all the time would have created a problem because the difference in her level of knowledge, skills and understanding was too high compared to that of the other children. I had to accept this difference and I let her work alone for part of the time on her butterfly project.

Melissa's education programme allows her to work with her peer group most of the time. She takes part in PE, music, singing, art and other general lessons, but is given differentiated lessons in mathematics which includes more investigation work. During reading time she selects her own books. As she is a fast worker, she is able to save quite a lot of time during regular work which she devotes to a special project. Melissa works on the project at home too. Her special project and its products provide her with an opportuntity to communicate with the teacher and other children. As the other children were curious and seemed very interested in the concept of a special project, Stephanie decided to offer an opportunity for all her children to pursue and work on their specially chosen project in their 'choosing' time and at home if they wished to do so.

Let us reflect for a moment on what Melissa's teacher has done here. She has acknowledged Melissa's special interests and her high ability in most areas, and provided her with opportunities to set her own expectations and to be productive. She is also using this opportunity to encourage other children to follow their own interests and carry out their own research. Parents and classroom assistants are encouraged to be involved. Think for a moment about what the alternative might have been. Melissa may have got frustrated if she was always forced to conform, to take part in the class numeracy lesson every day with its main focus on learning about numbers up to 20. The teacher would have felt guilty about making young Melissa do what she already knows, and ignoring her 'raised' hand for every question she asked the class to make sure that the others also had their chances.

Melissa loves school and looks forward to going back to school after weekends. This situation has not happened by accident. It is the result of a thoughtful and carefully devised strategy employed by her teacher.

Before moving on to the next section I will reiterate that the example used – Melissa's project – is by no means a single instance. My colleagues and I have found that spending a little time talking to children of all age groups about their interests and providing them with opportunities to follow them up in and outside school does enhance their motivation and help them to develop a positive attitude to learning.

Taking note of children's individual learning styles

All children have preferred learning styles and young gifted children are no exception. Taking note of children's individual learning styles would play an important part in maximising their learning opportunities. Research literature suggests that there is possible dominance of use of either the right or left brain and this can influence individual learning styles. Although a detailed discussion of how the right and left brain affect learning styles is beyond the scope of this book, it is useful to be aware of the generally accepted fact that all learners have preferred learning styles. Children's preferred learning styles may also be related to their sensory learning styles. Carbo *et al.* (1991) describe three styles: auditory, visual and tactile-kinaesthetic. The characterisitcs of each of these styles may be different. Auditory learners listen and follow instructions sequentially, visual learners may need to use pictures and other visual aids as stimuli and tactile learners prefer hands-on experiences. Some children may use a combination. Although it is difficult to identify accurately which of the styles is used by individual children, it is important that opportunities are provided for all three types of learners. For example, in the classroom we should have auditory equipment such as tape-recorders and ready-made recordings, visual aids such as film-strips, slides, pictures, videos and displays for the visual learners and construction equipment, cards, beads and counters for those who prefer to use tactile experiences.

When I discuss the topic of learning styles with teachers, they often point out that it is easier to take the learning styles into account in nursery classrooms for organisational purposes. It is true that as children get older, external pressures of recommended teaching styles are imposed on them; nevertheless the growing body of literature which supports the importance of taking account of children's individual learning styles for effective learning cannot be ignored. Thinking practically, say, most parts of a mathematics lesson adopt a whole-class teaching style. It is still possible to take a child's individual learning style into account by enabling him or her to use appropriate resources or to provide opportunties for some independent work for part of a mathematics lesson. A useful list of learning styles for observation and for planning activities is suggested by Beecher (1996). Based on Renzulli and Reis' Schoolwide Enrichment Model (Renzulli 1994), the following are some of the learning styles as preferred modes of instruction and teaching.

- *Project work*: A group of children work together on a project and the final product is shared with others. Teacher interaction is minimal.
- *Drill and recitation*: This is the traditional approach of teachers asking questions and children responding with answers. The responses are evaluated in terms of accuracy of facts.
- *Peer teaching*: This technique involves students as teachers of other students.
- *Discussion*: This consists of two-way interaction between the teacher and students and among students. It involves discussion and encourages children to think about relationships between ideas, and is a model for active participation.
- *Independent study*: This style involves individual students pursuing topics or areas of study on their own. This style is characterised by freedom from constant supervision, although some interaction is needed. The child selects a mode of study and presents a product.

How do you make an assessment of children's individual learning styles? With older children it is possible to ask them to respond to a list of preferred learning styles. With younger children close observation of how they respond to learning situations and discussions with them can often reveal their personal preferred style of learning.

Assessing children's individual strengths

The important role of assessment in making appropriate provision for young gifted children has been highlighted throughout this book. Assessment plays a central part in identifying the special needs of the children. The previous three sections of this chapter, which dealt with curriculum modification, identification of individual strengths and interests and the particular individual learning styles of children, highlight the need for teachers to be engaged in the ongoing formative assessment of children. Listening to what children say, observing what they do and evaluating the quality of their products will be integral to classroom practice. Although test results can provide summative, quantitative judgements on children's achievements, the quality of their work may be better assessed through tracking from the early years of schooling. Notes on what children know, can do and understand should be passed on from teacher to teacher so that learning experiences matched, special interests and development can be noted and appropriate provision made.

The following principles should help the process of gathering useful and high-quality formative assessment data.

- Authentic data on children's various strengths can only be obtained if appropriate opportunities are provided. For example, a particular strength in creative writing may be observed only if a child has an opportunity to produce an original piece of work. Similarly, a high level of interpersonal skills will hardly be demonstrated by a child who is seldom given an opportunity to work with other children.
- Assess children engaged in activities which are part of their normal classroom work.
- Let children share the assessment process by evaluating their strengths and areas for improvement. Most gifted children possess high metacognitive skills which can be usefully employed in self-assessment.
- Use closed and open-ended situations for assessing children's strengths. While closed questions can assess children's knowledge of facts and skills, open-ended questions and situations will help to illuminate the nature of their process skills and creative responses.
- Be wary of reasons which may make test results mask the true reflection of a child's ability. Fear of tests, excessive desire to please adults, a striving for perfection, language problems, illness or even bad moods can affect test results.
- Use portfolios for assessing children's ongoing development. My experience of being involved in helping children to develop portfolios suggests that they are an excellent way of recording children's special strengths and to assess their ongoing development. With this in mind I will share some of my thoughts on the role of portfolios for children.

Developing portfolios

What is a portfolio? According to Black and William (1998: 45)

> A portfolio is a collection of a student's work, usually constructed by a selection from larger corpus and often presented with reflective pieces written by the students justifying the selection.

With younger children, producing written evidence for the selection of items may be difficult, but verbal comments may be recorded by the teacher and notes kept. Developing a talent portfolio needs careful organisation. The intention is not to collect a random set of products. The purpose of a portfolio is to record the child's development and progress over time supported by tangible evidence wherever possible.

The best portfolios will be developmental. You may include a child's first pictures, a list of his or her favourite hobbies or events and examples of their best academic and artistic work. The contents will have dates and comments from teachers, children and other adults who may have been involved in the creation of a piece of work.

The process of selecting pieces of work in itself is useful. Ask the child why a certain piece of work was chosen and record the reasons. When I undertook research at the time of writing the book *Effective Teacher Assessment* (Mitchell and Koshy 1995) it was clear that children took great pride in collecting pieces of work for their portfolios. But initially, it needed some effort on the part of the teachers to train children to evaluate their work before selecting their best efforts. At their best, portfolios can provide the following benefits to children's learning and assessment:

- they increase the motivation to learn;
- children take ownership of their own learning;
- they celebrate children's achievement;
- with some training children will learn to be self-critical and reflect on their own learning;
- children are likely to strive to do better than their previous attempt rather than just compete with their peers;
- they provide the basis for homework and parents' evening discussions;
- the intrinsic satisfaction of constructing a record of achievement acts as a valuable reward and helps to develop self-esteem.

Children often show great pride in their portfolios. They also appreciate being given opportunities to show them to other people, including their parents on open days and evenings. Portfolios provide evidence of the way the school celebrates children's strengths and special interests which may not be easily demonstrated by recording test results or by awarding a National Curriculum-based Level of Achievement.

Involving adults in the child's learning process

The role of parents and teachers in both the identification and nurturing of children's special abilities has permeated the whole of the book. This section is especially devoted to a consideration of the important role played by all the adults in the fulfilment of young talents. In Chapter 3 I referred to Vygotsky's idea of a child's Zone of Proximal Development (ZPD) and how adult guidance can play an important part in supporting children to demonstrate their ZPD. The message is that when working with challenging concepts, children will perform at a more advanced level than their current level of development provided there is the right kind of guidance. Vygotsky's (1978: 86) explanation is worthy of consideration:

> The zone of proximal development defines those functions which have not yet matured but are in the process of maturation, functions that will mature tomorrow but are currently in an embryonic state. These functions could be termed as 'buds' or 'flowers' of development rather than the 'fruits' of development. The actual developmental level characterises mental development retrospectively, while the zone of proximal development characterises mental development prospectively.

Sensitive and informed adult guidance is vital for children's development and all adults who work with children should be skilled in the process of moving children's learning forward. This includes teachers, parents, classroom assistants and classroom helpers. They should have a shared understanding of the attributes associated with young gifted children, methods of identification of children's special strengths, the value of good questioning skills and the nature of children's thinking processes.

In a collaborative project with a Local Education Authority our centre for able children at the university set up some structures to support all the adults who were involved in educating gifted youngsters. Three particular groups of people were offered support and the outcomes were evaluated as 'effective' by all those who participated in the activities. The support offered to the three different groups of adults was in the following format:

- Teachers as researchers
- In-service support for classroom assistant and support staff
- Guidance for parents.

Teachers as researchers

A group of infant and nursery teachers were sponsored by their schools and local education authorities to carry out small-scale research into aspects of gifted education with reference to younger children. Each teacher selected a topic which was relevant to his or her situation and set up a programme of either an investigation into existing practices and possible ways of modifying them or an intervention programme and a way to evaluate its effectiveness. The project lasted for eight months during which detailed notes and journals were kept. Examples of topics were:

- The nature of children's responses to learning experiences in both 'set' and 'mixed ability' groups.
- The effect of enhanced parental involvement on children's attitudes and achievement.
- Structures for incorporating special projects within curriculum planning.
- Children's level of knowledge of content prior to being taught.
- Children's perceptions of their particular strengths.
- Parental expectations and children's attitudes.
- Modifying questioning styles.

All the teacher-researchers presented their findings at a local conference. As well as being of interest to all those who attended the conference, it was obvious that the benefits derived by the teachers from a focused study were significant. Recording their experiences, philosophies and tensions, collecting samples of children's work, analysing them and sharing the data with colleagues helped to make adjustments to what and how children were taught. Adopting the process of ongoing observation, discussion and reflection of what children were doing, the nursery teachers felt that they were following similar principles to those of the successful *Reggio Emilia* programme for pre-school children which originated in Italy.

In-service support for classroom assistants and support staff

A series of talks and workshops were arranged for classroom assistants. They were asked to carry out focused observation of children and to identify their relative strengths. Some sessions addressed the role of questioning in extending children's thinking, the importance of creating a rich environment for learning, how to encourage problem-solving and so on. These sessions were found to be very valuable by the course participants and according to post-course evaluations from class teachers, there was strong evidence that what was 'learned' by classroom assistants and support staff was implemented in the classroom. My own feeling is that in order to be effective practitioners, all those who deal with young children need to develop a shared understanding of the principles by which the school operates.

Guidance for parents

The third strand of support offered as part of the collaborative project was designed to develop parents' understanding of aspects of identification of special abilities and how to respond. The importance of achieving a balance between encouraging children to make the most of their abilities and exercising excessive pressure to do well by pushing them too hard to achieve unrealistic targets was emphasised.

Ways in which parents can support schools in both the identification process in helping them to achieve their full potential were looked at. The following list highlights a set of recommendations compiled by the parents for a leaflet on the basis of talks, literature search and guided discussions. The list provides suggestions as to how parents can be empowered to support the development of young gifted children. Parents can help by:

- sharing with the school information on children's aptitudes and interests;
- offering to work with the school sharing the same philosophies;
- providing feedback to the teacher on attitudes to specific work and projects;
- sharing the development of the child's talent portfolio;
- not showing over-anxiety;
- accepting that ability may be 'all round' or in a particular domain;
- encouraging children to talk about their activities and special interests;
- attending school workshops and meetings to share information on aspects of giftedness.

Useful guidance for developing children's special interests

Finally here is some guidance for those who are involved in educating young gifted children which was put together by the course participants. Many of the ideas were based on the guidance notes from The National Centre on the Gifted and Talented provided by Marcia A. Delcourt.

Children's early interests in activities and collections should always be encouraged. Although hobbies and interests change over time, there is evidence to suggest that developing a passion for pursuing an interest helps children to make sustained efforts in an area of learning and be engaged in meaningful enquiry and research. This enhances their motivation and productivity. Some world-class experts who have made outstanding contributions became interested in particular topics when they were very young. Whatever the nature of the new-found interest is, and strange as it may sometimes seem, adults should encourage children to visit relevant places, rent or buy equipment and make efforts to enable them to meet children with the same interest as often as possible.

Show interest in children's interests, talk to them about it, share reading about it and if possible find a mentor – someone who knows about the topic – who is willing to share his or her knowledge. Local secondary schools and higher education institutions may be very willing to support the budding talents of a youngster. According to Gardner (1993), many creative and inventive people talk about a person who significantly influenced their paths of enquiry and fulfilment.

Encourage children to take their product to school and share it with their teachers, and if possible with other children too. Dated evidence of outstanding performance which is included in the child's portfolio may be used to monitor development and help to identify the nature of any support needed.

Considering organisational issues

During my in-service courses and workshops on provision for younger children, three of the most commonly asked questions are:

1 If a child shows an advanced cognitive level in the early years, is there a case for early entry to the infant school?
2 What are your views about acceleration?
3 What is the difference between acceleration and enrichment with regard to the curriculum offered?

Each of the questions relate to how we organise children's learning, and there are no hard and fast rules for guidance. I always emphasise that each child is unique and how we deal with a particular child will depend on many factors. What is important is that we understand these terms – early entry, acceleration and enrichment programmes – and their implications so that we can make informed decisions when we need to. To enable the readers to enhance their understanding of these issues, I will discuss each of these in the following section.

Early entry

The age of entry to infant school within our education system is based on age. It is up to the individual schools to decide which term he or she starts school before age five. It is not that there is anything magical about being aged five, it is more of an administrative convenience.

Increasingly, schools are being approached by parents who wish to enrol their children on the basis of their advanced mental alertness, precocity or a display of a high level of knowledge and understanding of concepts. Sometimes parents have their children tested privately, often by a psychologist, who may assess his or her cognitive ability to be exceptional. This assessment is normally based on IQ testing which may reveal that a child is functioning at a much higher level than that of other children of their age. Whatever the basis for the application for early entry, the school has to make a decision.

What are the arguments usually put forward for early entry being a useful strategy? Consider the following:

- A child who is very advanced for his or her age may be performing at the cognitive level of a much older child. Questions and activities provided in the classroom may be too simple for the child who in turn may be put off learning.
- It is unfair to make a gifted child wait a year just because of a regulation based on a date for entry.
- It is better to allow a gifted child to start school early, so that the child becomes used to working with a peer group of children right from the start rather than being subjected to being moved up later.

What are the possible difficulties with early entry?

- A child who may be cognitively advanced may not have the social and emotional maturity necessary to be placed with older children. Waiting a year or two can make a significant difference.
- Some parents may push a case for early entry for all sorts of reasons and make exaggerated claims about their children's ability.
- Assessment of children's ability and suitability to be placed with older children will need very careful thought and much discussion between parents, teachers and possibly other experts.
- What is required for a gifted child is not 'year skipping' and teaching the content designed for an older age group, but a differentiated curriculum which provides challenge. Early entry may be a temporary solution, but what is needed is for teachers to develop sound differentiation strategies.

There are no hard and fast rules for early entry to school. The child's academic competence, emotional maturity and physical size need to be taken into account before making decisions. Research has not shown any serious adverse effects for early entry to schools. My own personal view is that if we mean one year 'early' and if it is done very carefully, and kept under review, I cannot see many problems.

Acceleration

Early entry into school may be viewed as a form of *acceleration*. I have heard the word *acceleration* being used to mean different things to different people. One explanation of the word, in the context of educating gifted children, is to let them learn new material normally taught to children in a higher age group. This may be done either by letting the children stay with their peer group or by moving them up to a class of older children. The word is more commonly used to refer to the latter scenario. In both cases new content is taught. Most schools which use this strategy do so because it offers an organisationally simple way of matching teaching material to the cognitive level of the child. Critics who express concern do so based on two grounds. First, a child whose thinking capability is qualitatively superior needs opportunities for in-depth thinking and exploration. Secondly, making children go up to a class of children who are more than a year older may create problems if the child's emotional maturity has not developed at the same rate as their cognitive ability. In some cases, I know of children who were very distressed because of their smaller size. Not being selected for football or for teams by the other children have also been cited as causing concern for young children who were placed with children in an older class.

Again, any decisions about acceleration need to be taken with great care. Everyone involved – the teacher, headteacher, parents and the child in some form or another – must consider the advantages and disadvantages of the process. If in doubt, delay the decision and think again. There are many ways in which a child's learning needs may be met without resorting to *radical acceleration*, a term used to describe moving children up to a class where children are several years older.

Enrichment

In the context of educating the gifted child, the word *enrichment* is used to mean opportunities for in-depth thinking and exploration. If planned well, it is way of working which excites children. Enrichment activities will undoubtedly lead to learning new content. For example, a child researching for a project will come across new knowledge and use it in context. Enrichment activities involve more cognitive processes such as analysis, problem-solving and evaluation. A word of caution here: any enrichment activity given to children needs to be monitored. While it is easy to assess what a child has learned in the acceleration model of learning, what has been learned through an enrichment activity is harder to assess. Quality of the thought processing and products needs to be considered.

Summary

In this chapter we considered ways in which we organise learning. First, we considered aspects of curriculum modification including ideas of streamlining elements of the curriculum which have been mastered by the child already. The importance of encouraging children to follow individual projects and taking note of their learning styles were considered. Issues of assessment and the role of adults in helping children to fulfil their potential were explored. Organisational issues which are specific in the context of educating younger gifted children were also discussed.

5 Subject-specific provision in mathematics, English and ICT

In Chapters 3 and 4 we covered aspects of effective classroom provision for young gifted children. In Chapter 3, I discussed some general strategies for making a difference for these children in the classroom. Chapter 4 addressed specific ways in which the achievement and self-esteem of individual children could be enhanced. Both chapters should offer guidance to teachers in all aspects of the curriculum. This chapter, devoted to subject-specific provision, should ideally address aspects of teaching of all subjects, but it was felt that it would be beyond the scope of this book to achieve this objective. Therefore, I have selected three subjects as the main focus of this chapter. The reason for selecting mathematics and English for special consideration was twofold. First, teachers consider these two subject as the two basic curriculum areas. Second, there have been many requests from teachers, since the introduction of the National Numeracy and Literacy Strategies, for guidance on aspects of provision for these two areas of the curriculum. I chose ICT as the third subject because it not only offers opportunities for enhancing curriculum provision in all subjects, but also makes a significant contribution in developing a number of other desirable skills of communication, processes such as reasoning and problem-solving and applying higher-order thinking skills such as analysis, synthesis and evaluation. Within the framework of development of Multiple Intelligences which this book promotes, aspects of English and mathematics would fall within linguistic, logical-mathematical and spacial intelligences and practical applications of ICT should enhance all seven intelligences.

Sections of this chapter dealing with aspects of teaching mathematics and English to gifted young children are structured in such a way that they would address the following issues:

- attributes which would indicate a high aptitude for the subject;
- implications of the listed attributes for classroom provision;
- strategies which could be adopted to ensure effective teaching of the subject.

The section on ICT will be considered in a different format. This will be presented as a means of enhancing the learning opportunities for highly able children. Exemplification of strategies will be provided for all three sections.

As we are about to focus on identification and fulfilment of potential in two subject areas, I would like to direct the readers' attention to the cautionary note given in the guidance from the DfES (2000a: 2) for teaching mathematics and English to able children:

> High ability does not always result in high attainment. Able children may conceal their ability because of social pressures, becoming reticent in class and difficult to involve. Attainment can be uneven, for example an outstanding reader may produce writing which is superficial and undeveloped. In Key Stage 1, some pupils develop an early proficiency in reading using sight vocabulary and contextual cues, but lack phonic skills, others may have the ability to produce language and ideas for composing text, but experience problems in transcription.

Baseline assessment, using multiple sources for assessing children's ability – parental views, tests, portfolios and observation notes – described in Chapter 2 should provide a more accurate judgement of children's potential.

Teaching able mathematicians

The past five years have witnessed some developments in mathematics teaching. International comparisons highlighted concerns about British children's mathematical achievement, a National Numeracy Strategy was launched and a framework for teaching mathematics was issued. The main aim of the recent developments listed above is to raise the level of achievement in mathematics. This has obvious implications for teaching mathematically promising pupils. As part of the recent national emphasis on the education of gifted and talented pupils, a number of publications and other resources have been provided to support subject-specific provision. They include guidance on teaching numeracy to able children (DfES 2000a) a pack of mathematical challenges for able mathematicians at Key Stages 1 and 2 (DfES 2000b), World-Class tests in mathematics (see Resources), development of advanced mathematics centres which include a mathematical enrichment programme based at Brunel University and a training materials video (from QCA, see Resources) which provide exemplars of good practice. Although some of the resources listed are targeted at older children, they should offer guidance for teaching younger children, either by using the ideas as they are or by adapting them, as mathematical ability is not age-related.

Identification of mathematically able children

I am often told that mathematical ability is the easiest to spot and provide for. If our perception of mathematical ability is in terms of children producing correct answers to numeral tasks, and provision is described in terms of giving children harder sums, this may be the case. In order to identify a high level of mathematical promise we also need to look for other attributes. To make a start in thinking about issues of identification, it is useful to consider a research-based list produced by Sheffield

(1994) which should provide indicators of high mathematical ability. Mathematically promising children demonstrate the following:

- Early and keen awareness, curiosity, and understanding about quantitative information.
- Ability to perceive, visualise and generalise patterns and relationships.
- Ability to reason analytically, deductively and inductively.
- Ability to reverse a reasoning process and to switch methods easily but not impulsively.
- Ability to work with mathematical concepts in fluent, flexible and creative ways.
- Energy and persistence in solving difficult problems.
- Ability to transfer learning to novel situations.
- Tendency to formulate mathematical questions, not just answer them.
- Ability to organise and work with data in a variety of ways and to disregard irrelevant data.

Sheffield draws our attention to the fact that the above list does not include the ability to compute rapidly and accurately. She maintains that while some mathematically gifted pupils may have this ability, it is not a necessary or sufficient characteristic to identify mathematical giftedness. In fact, many mathematically very able pupils are impatient with details and do not care to spend time on computation. They are often anxious to get on to the important aspects of the problem.

The list presented above has many of the attributes listed by the Russian psychologist Krutetskii (1976), who carried out extensive research into mathematical giftedness. Mathematical promise is often shown in the early years of a child. In this context it is particularly relevant to note Straker's (1982) support for identifying mathematically able pupils in the first years of schooling. She maintains that children may show interest in stories and rhymes which include numbers, may have a particular ability for creating and detecting patterns, sort by sophisticated attributes, and excel in construction work and solving jigsaw puzzles.

Strategies for effective provision

A close look at the attributes of mathematically promising children listed in the previous section provides us with a framework for targeting provision. In order to meet the needs of mathematically able children we should provide them with a teaching programme which offers opportunities to learn more advanced concepts, and one which is qualitatively different and encourages the development of processes. Younger children are naturally curious and ask many questions. This feature may be used to encourage curiosity and creativity. One must also remember that children show varied levels of mathematical ability. Some may show exceptional ability, as was demonstrated by the famous mathematician Gauss, who is said to have generated a strategy, at the age of seven, to add all the numbers from 1 to 100 by pairing them. He added 1 and 100, 2 and 99, 3 and 98 and so on, and multiplied the total of each pair by the number of pairs – 50. He also generalised the findings so that he could find the totals of any set of numbers. Such mathematical precocity may be unusual, but the opportunities must be made available for such children to show their potential.

In the next section, I will present a set of strategies as well as some examples of good practice, which I believe will provide a square deal for our younger gifted mathematicians. These are only briefly described here due to constraints of space, but are presented in more detail along with many other suggestions of support in my book *Teaching Mathematics to Able Children* (Koshy 2001). So, how do we meet the needs of the younger mathematically gifted child?

Creating a mathematics environment

In the context of setting up interest centres to encourage the development of special interests and aptitudes, I provided a list in Chapter 3 of what may be included in the mathematics corner. We should provide children with a variety of structured and free-play materials to explore and experiment. These would include construction toys, Lego, regular and irregular shapes, jigsaws, a collection of dice, calculators, number lines, and sets of pictorial and verbal puzzles. Books with a mathematics focus and mathematics vocabulary books should be displayed. Let children play with the materials, but there should also be periods when an adult may observe the children and ask them to explain what they are doing, encouraging them to use the correct mathematical vocabulary. I suggest that the adults working with children should spend some time together considering the kinds of questions to ask and activities to suggest. The aim of the interventions is to extend children's thinking, help them to refine their mathematical ideas and develop a positive attitude towards the subject.

Asking the right kinds of questions

The role of questions in extending children's thinking has been discussed previously. In this section it is further discussed within the context of mathematics learning. Questions which ask *why* and *how, what do you notice,* and *what if* ... are more likely to encourage children to apply mathematical processes of reasoning, making conjectures, hypothesising and generalising. For example, the following questions will encourage higher order thinking. Using a collection of normal six-sided dice:

- What do you notice about the numbering on dice?
- Do the opposite sides always add up to seven?
- If I place one die on top of another, can you work out what the hidden numbers are?
- How many different ways can you get a total of 18 using four dice?
- What is the name of the shape of a die? Can you draw a net to show me?

We must also encourage children to ask questions. Some time ago, I was working with a group of six-year-old children on an investigation of 'Smarties'. I asked them to think of questions we could ask about tubes of Smarties. They were quite lost and explained to me that *'it is the teacher who always asks the questions, not the children!'* But after a little encouragement they did ask some very good questions. Where the habit of asking questions is established, children do ask some very profound questions. An example of this comes to mind when a six-year-old asked why we always grouped numbers in 'tens' and what would happen to 'adding up' sums if we did not group in 'tens'. An individual project on working in a different base, base 8, as they may do in Spiderland, was suggested and taken up. The project took some time to complete, but it was an enriching experience for the child.

Organising mathematics lessons flexibly

One of the ways in which a differentiated programme can be provided is through flexible styles of organisation. Four styles of organisation may be used which should provide a differentiated input.

They are:

1 Whole-class mixed ability teaching.
2 Working in groups or 'sets' of similar ability.
3 Working with a class of older children.
4 Working independently.

Most classrooms use all four types of organisation. Each has advantages and serves different purposes. Each of the organisational styles also needs guidance to make good use of the strategy. For example, during whole-class teaching of a mixed ability class, meeting the intellectual needs of a very able mathematician is a challenge. Some differentiation is possible with targeted questioning, but for a child who is way ahead of others in his or her knowledge of facts and skills as well as the level of conceptual understanding, differentiated questions may only partially help the situation. Working in 'setted' groups has the advantage of reducing the range of ability within a group, and this kind of organisation allows children to interact with children who may have developed more sophisticated levels of thinking and have a wider mathematical vocabulary. Working with older children is another way of providing for a child who is working at a significantly higher level than the other children, although arguments against this type of provision are often put forward based on physical aspects of size and emotional immaturity of the child.

Working independently for part of the time and with guidance from an adult or older child who has the necessary understanding of mathematics is often suggested as an effective strategy for children who are motivated and have a strong passion for pursuing mathematical enquiries. My own suggestion is that any organisational structure one adopts must take the child's interest and development into account and should form an integral part of a sound mathematics teaching programme.

Providing enrichment activities

Enrichment is often used to mean encouraging in-depth thinking and this is usually achieved by an investigative style of working. Suitable activities are selected to enable children to investigate ideas and develop mathematical processes.

Types of suitable activities

USING ACTIVITIES WITH DIFFERENTIATED OUTCOMES

Give the children a sheet of paper with an arithmagon on it and ask them to investigate different ways of finding a solution (Figure 5.1). Listen to the discussion.

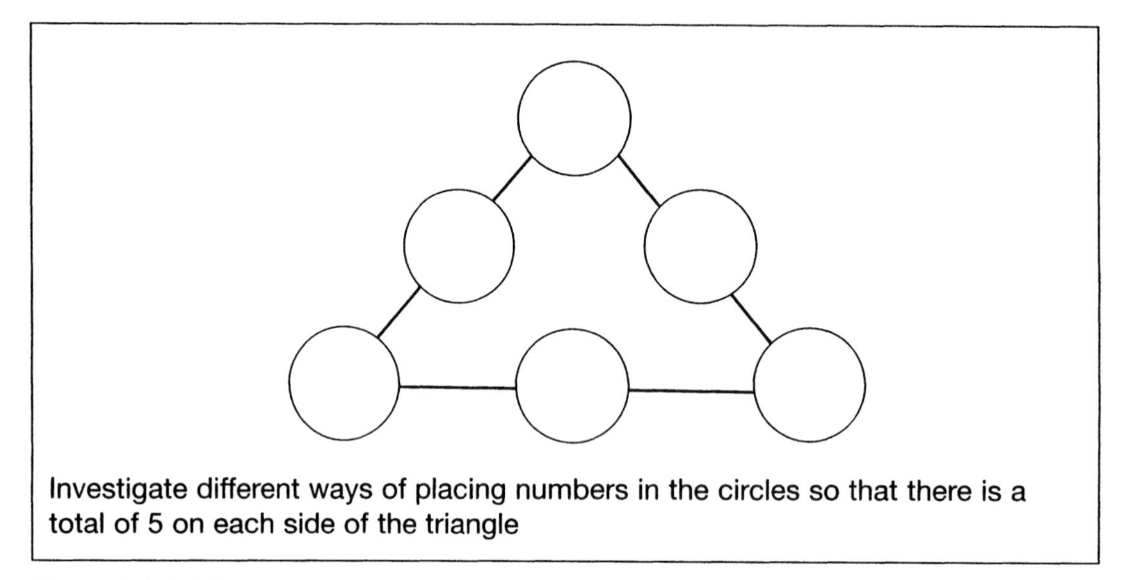

Figure 5.1 Arithmagon

This activity has a range of outcomes. It generates some solutions, but it can also be used to encourage systematic work which will generate 20 solutions. Children may use different methods and resources and generate their own hypotheses and solutions.

The second activity 'Hoops' in Figure 5.2a and b (ATM 1993) – *How many ways can three people arrange themselves in the hoops?* – can generate a solution and a range of strategies and ways of recording.

Questions can be asked to extend the challenge:

- What if there are two people and three hoops?
- What if there are four people and four hoops ?

WORKING ON PUZZLES

The DfES (2000b) publication, *Mathematical Challenges for Able pupils in Key Stages 1 and 2'* provides a wealth of puzzles that can be used in a variety of ways. As the notes suggest, puzzles can 'help children to work systematically, sort and classify information, develop reasoning, predicting, testing hypotheses and evaluating the solutions'. When working on puzzles we can encourage children to extend their thinking by asking more questions. Posing their own questions is one very effective way of extending children's mathematical thinking.

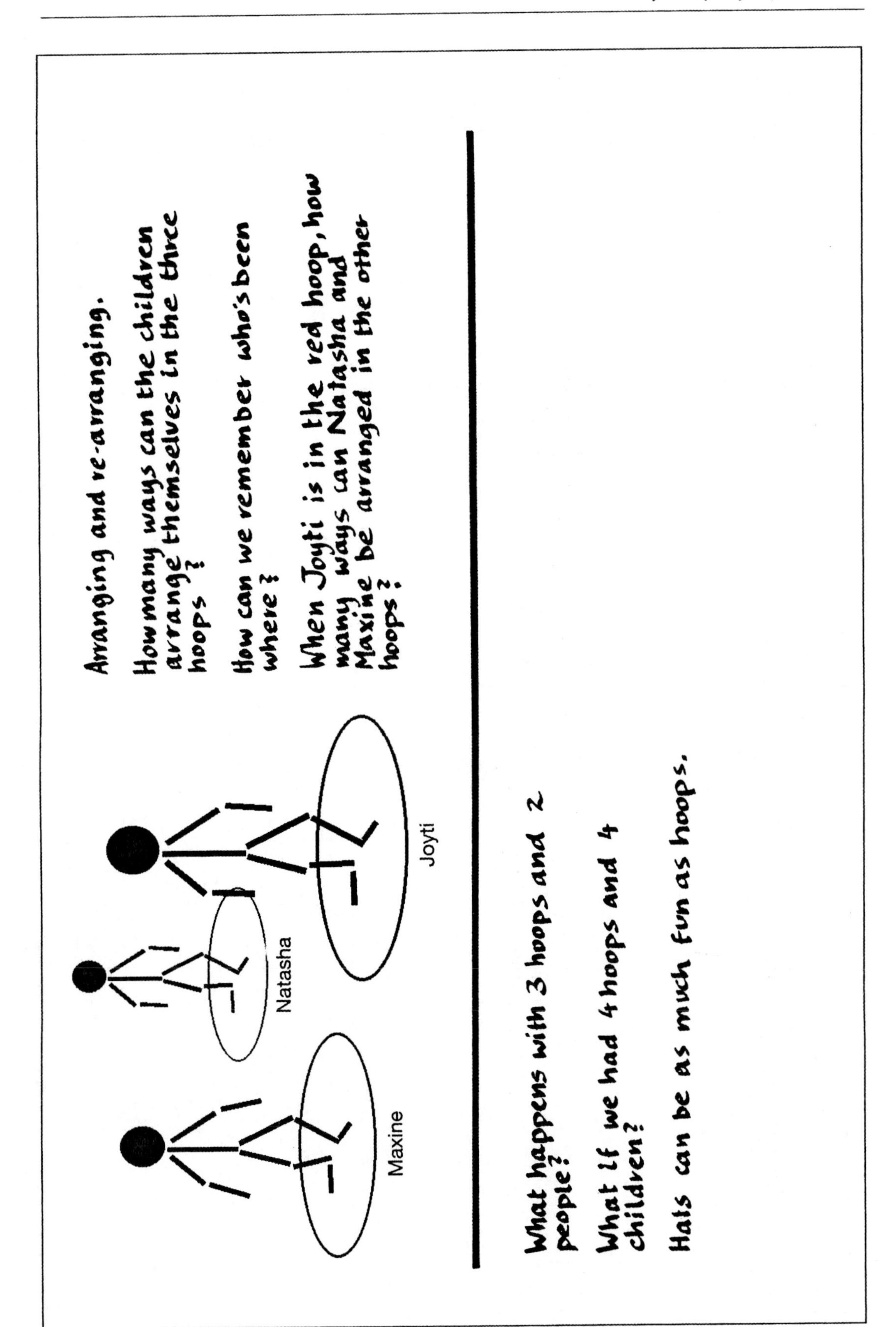

Figure 5.2a The Hoops Problem

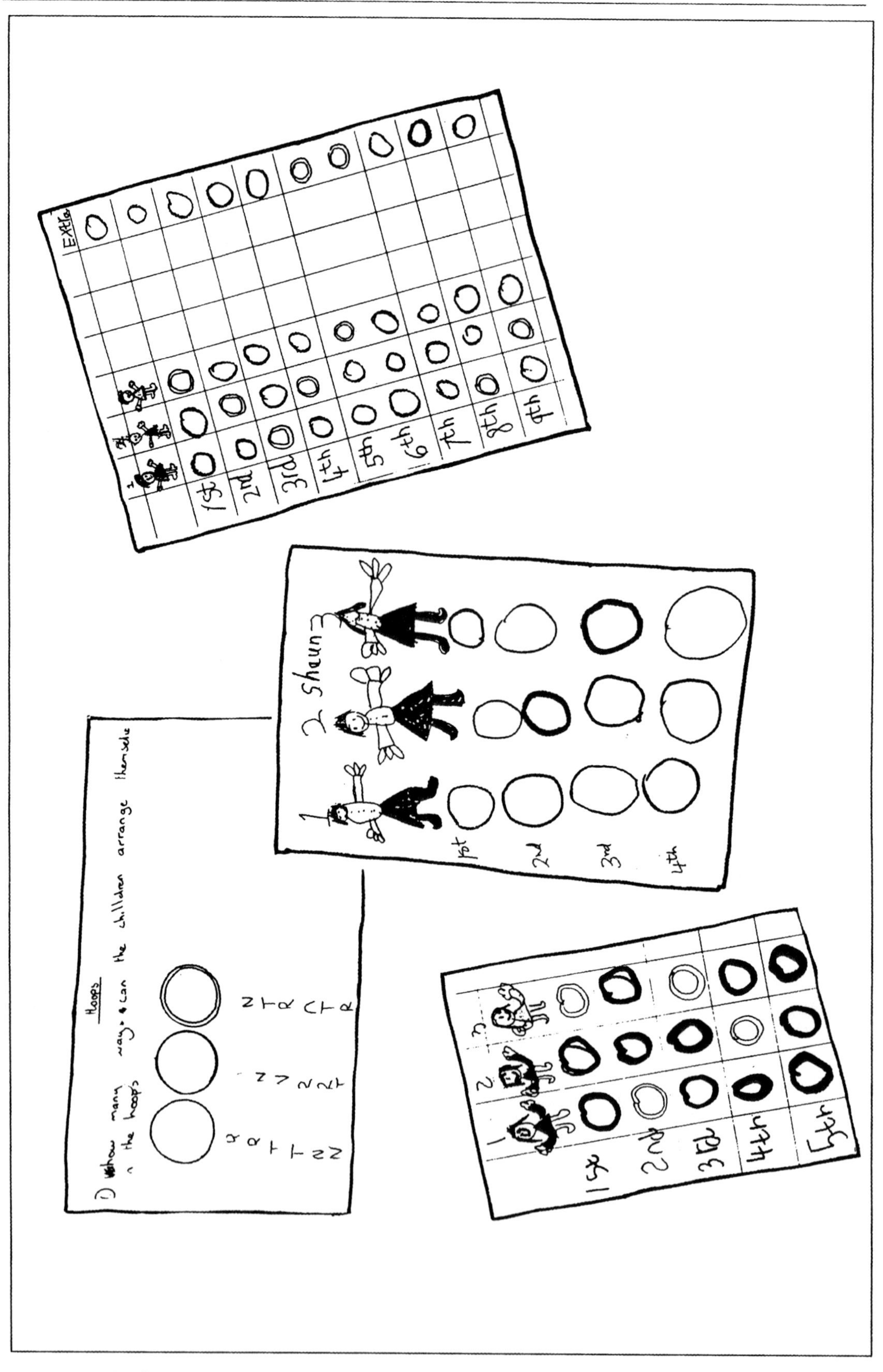

Figure 5.2b The Hoops Problem

Using activities with potential for generalisation

Children of all age groups are capable of generalisations at different levels. To tackle the following 'Build a Tower' activity in a Year 2 class, in (see Figure 5.3), different children used different strategies and some attempted generalisations.

The strategies used were as follows.

One group built four- and five-cube tall towers and recorded the number of cubes needed. Another group, with a little prompting from the teacher, recorded the results as:

Height of tower	Number of cubes
2	4
3	9
4	16
5	25

They spotted a pattern that the number of cubes were going up in a sequence + 5, + 7, + 9 and so on and a more able group, with some encouragement from the teacher, noticed that there was a relationship between the height of the tower and the number of cubes needed. With the help of a calculator more examples were tried and a generalisation was written. New words, symbols and a new operation – square numbers and square root and appropriate procedures and symbols for finding the 'square root' using a calculator – were taught.

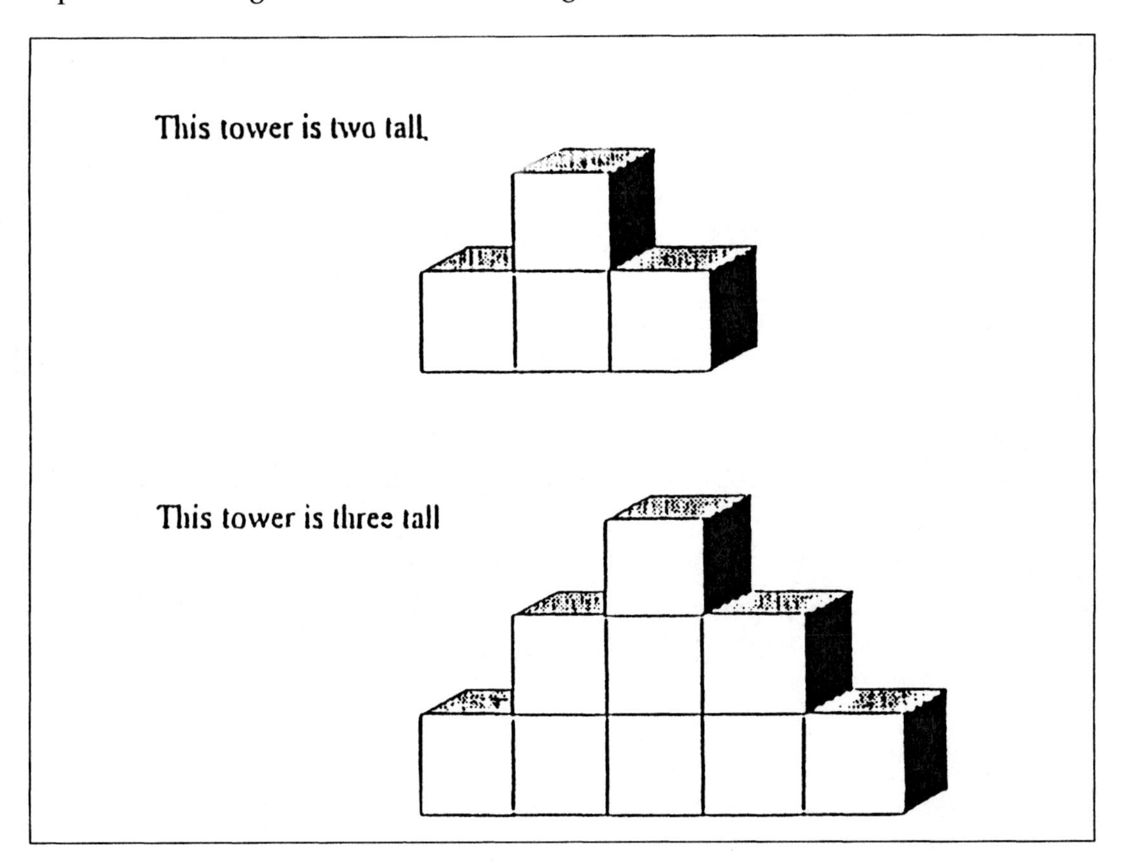

Figure 5.3 Build a Tower activity

Letting children reflect on their work

The value of children reflecting on their work – in other words, exercising their metacognitive skills – has already been referred to. Here is an example of a group of Year 2 children working on consecutive numbers. After a mental starter focusing on discussing consecutive numbers, a differentiated task was given to the whole class for the main lesson. All but one group was asked to work on the question:

> *Which of the numbers from 1 to 20 can you make by adding consecutive numbers?* A group of able pupils was given a related but more open-ended task, a sheet of A3 paper and coloured pens.
> *Find out what you can about adding consecutive numbers and write down some of your discoveries and present them to the class during the plenary.*

During the plenary many discoveries were presented by the children. Examples were:

- If you add two consecutive numbers the answer is always odd.
- If you add three consecutive numbers the total is odd or even depending on the number you start with.
- You cannot make all the numbers from 1 to 20 by adding consecutive numbers. We are still wondering why this is and if there is a pattern which will tell us the reason ... and so on.

Encouraging investigative work

One of my favourite activities for younger children is the 'Ladybird' activity (Figure 5.4). If the ladybird likes to have the same number of spots on both sides what numbers could she use? This was investigated by a group of four- and five-year-olds. The level of discussion and mathematical thinking was quite impressive (Figure 5.5).

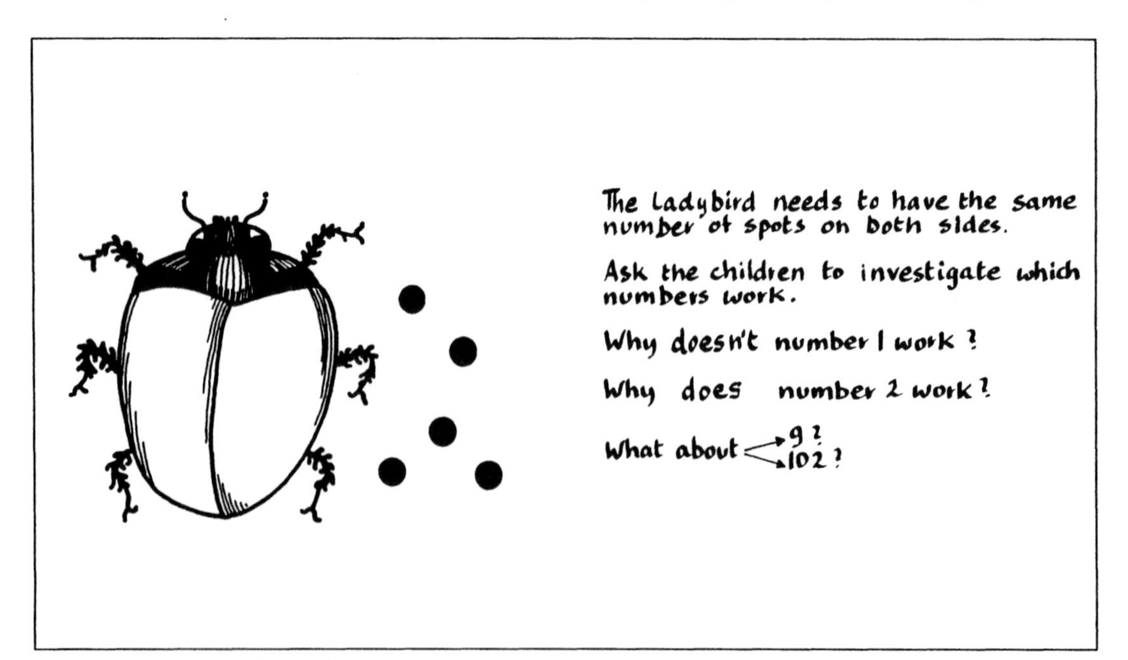

Figure 5.4 The Ladybird activity

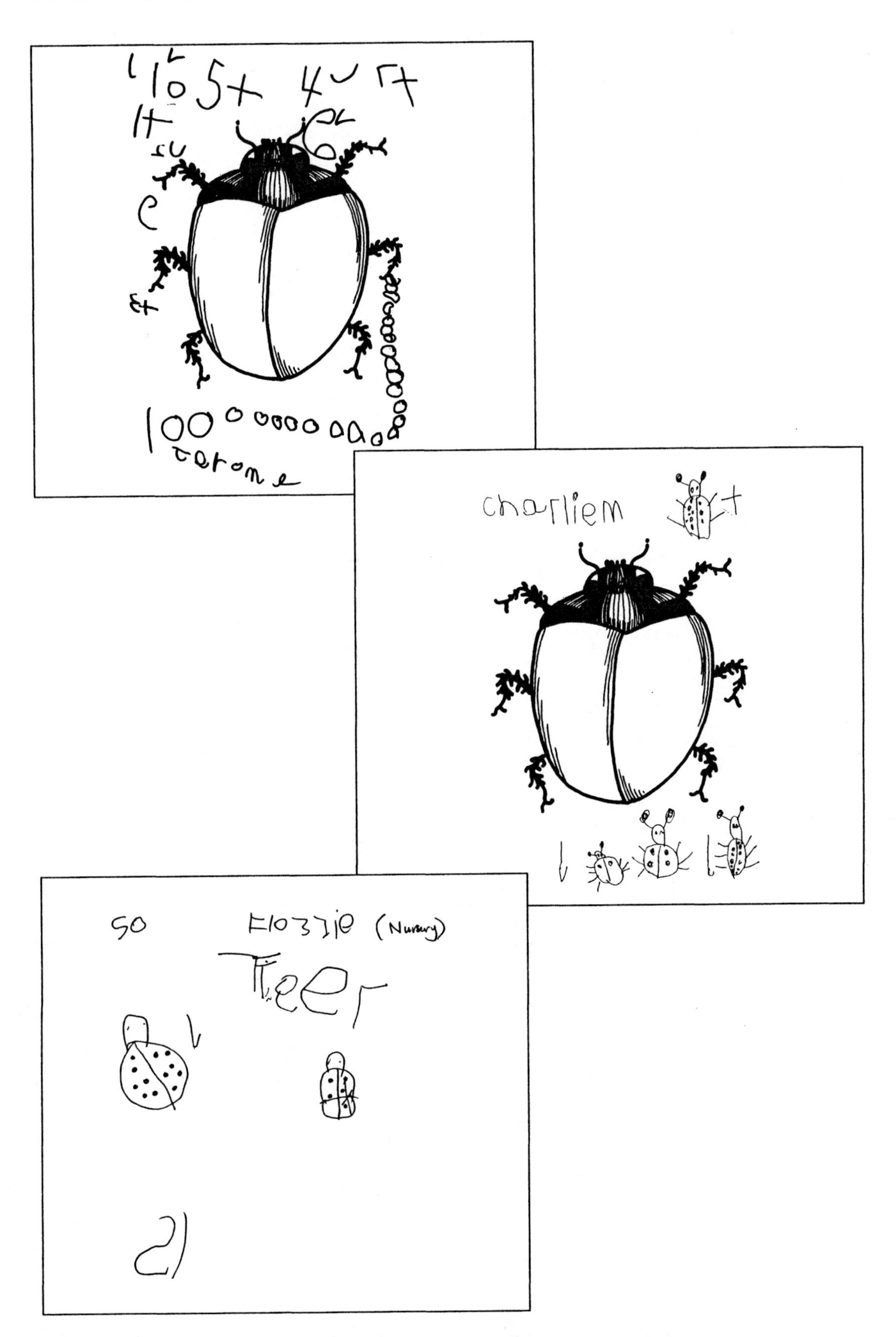

Figure 5.5 Results of the Ladybird activity (ages 4–5)

A few years ago, I worked with a group of six-year-olds using the same investigation to be included in a publication by ATM (1993). The level of participation and initiative taken by the children, as can be seen in Figure 5.6, impressed me a great deal. Young children are capable of making connections, exploring number properties and producing systematic work when they are given opportunities to do so.

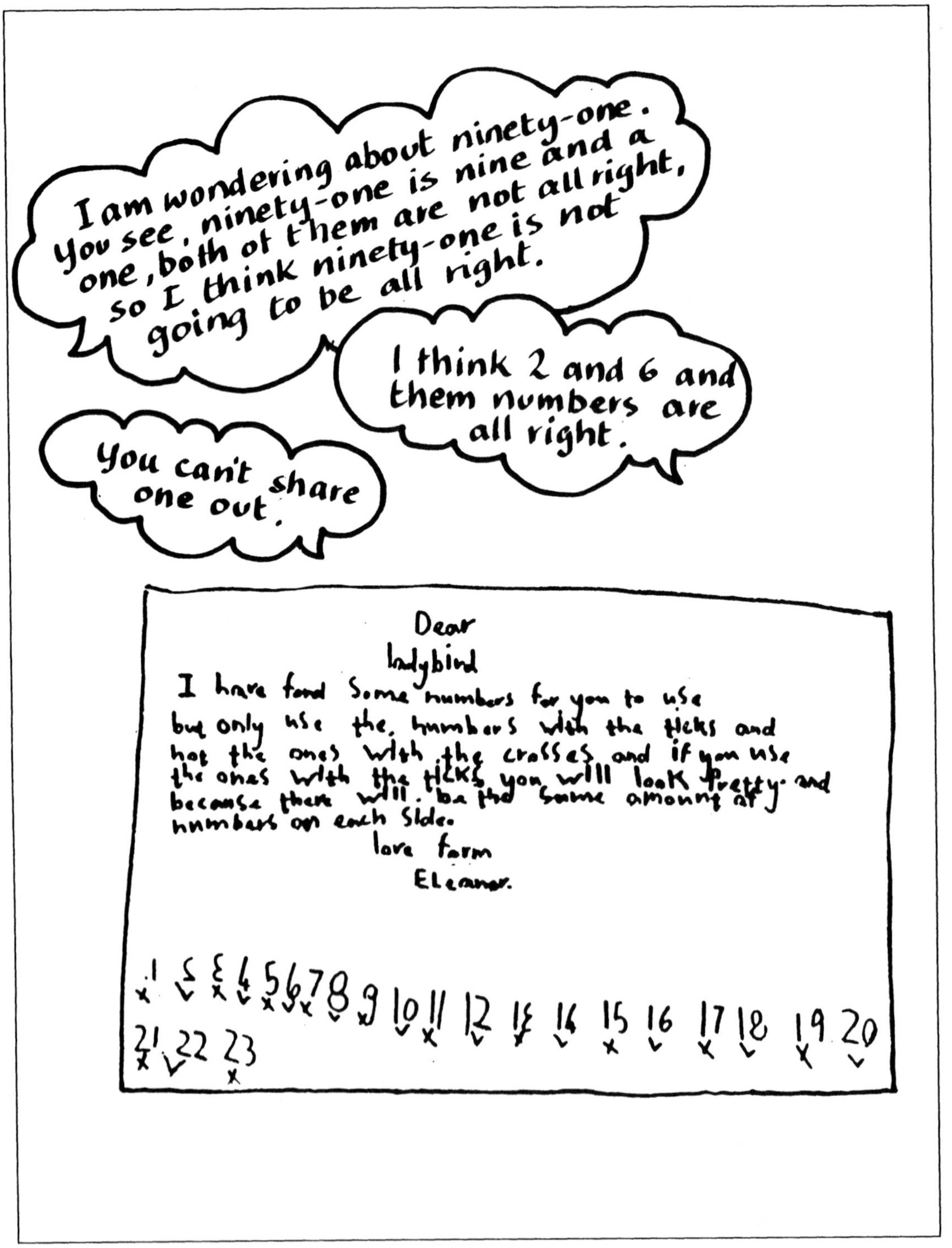
I am wondering about ninety-one. You see, ninety-one is nine and a one, both of them are not all right, so I think ninety-one is not going to be all right.
I think 2 and 6 and them numbers are all right.
You can't share one out.
Dear
ladybird
I have fond Some numbers for you to use
but only use the numbers with the ticks and
not the ones with the crosses and if you use
the ones with the ticks you will look pretty and
because there will be the Same amount of
numbers on each Side.
love form
Eleanor.
1 2 3 4 5 6 7 8 9 10 11 12 13 14 15 16 17 18 19 20
21 22 23

Figure 5.6 Results of the Ladybird activity (age 6)

MOVING AWAY FROM THE TRADITIONAL FORMAT

Young, able mathematicians enjoy the challenges offered to them in non-traditional formats. For example, I found that the level of motivation was high when I asked a group of seven-year-olds to pretend that they were teachers and to mark some work produced by other children (not from their class). They were asked to look at each question and see if the answers were correct; and if they were wrong, to think of reasons why the mistakes were made. Similarly, the level of motivation and participation was high when some six-year-olds were asked to judge if the following statements shown below were likely or unlikley. Calculators were made available if needed.

- You have been alive 200 months.
- A person can walk 100 miles per hour.
- Your teacher's foot is 10cm long.
- The tallest teddy bear in the class is 5 metres.

Young, gifted mathematicians are often capable of sophisticated thought processes. I have seen young children working on *'Books of shapes', 'My own book of puzzles and solutions', 'Would you rather book'*; and investigating ideas such as:

- Would you rather have a handful of 10 penny pieces or 20 penny pieces?
- Would you rather have your pocket money as 10 pence per day for two weeks or start with 1p on the first day, 2p on the second day, 4p on the third day, doubling it each day and have the total for two weeks?
- Would you prefer to do addition or subtraction sums? Explain why.

USING ICT

Some of the most challenging work I have seen in infant classrooms was done with the aid of ICT. Calculators enable children to have access to larger numbers when solving problems, and data-handling packages help them to test their hypotheses and present evidence. Websites such as 'ENRICH' and world-class test sites (see Resources) offer children opportunities for problem-solving. I have included a more detailed discussion of the use of ICT for challenging mathematically able children later in this chapter.

Teaching children with a high ability in English

Parents of gifted children have often told me that they noticed their children's special talents in language reading very early on in their children's lives. Early reading of shop signs and words, a fascination for words and sounds are often mentioned as indicators of talent in language. Within the framework of Gardner's Multiple Intelligences this special ability is classified under linguistic intelligence. Indicators of this were discussed in Chapter 2. In this section, I have listed the attributes which should help us to identify special strengths in English. Since the introduction of the National Literacy Strategy, there has been a significant improvement in children's achievement in general. But the question is whether the strategy has enhanced opportunities for the able language user. In the absence of any published research we have to rely on feedback from teachers who have put forward mixed reactions. There are many who feel that the focus on literacy has provided a context for enhancing the quality of work in English, while others have expressed concern that the time constraints have imposed limitations on certain types of work – extended writing is given as one example. One positive aspect is that, for the first time, schools in England and Wales are issued with some guidance on teaching English to able children (see Resources).

In this section, we will consider some attributes often demonstrated by young, gifted language learners and the implications of these for classroom provision. Some strategies for providing more challenging experiences will also be explored.

Identifying the able language learner

The guidelines from the DfES(2000a) offer the the following as attributes of children who are able in literacy. They:

- can orchestrate the various reading cues at an early age;
- are active readers who can generalise from their reading experience;
- latch on quickly to the conventions of different types of writing;
- think in original ways and experiment with new styles;
- manipulate language, sentence structure and punctuation, use apt terminology and a varied vocabulary.

In the context of a research project entitled *Bright Challenge* (Casey and Koshy 2001) through observation of a number of young children who were identified as high achievers in English we found that these children:

- are able to express ideas and present arguments;
- had a wide vacabulary;
- are likely to enjoy reading a variety of books – fiction and non-fiction;
- are sometimes reluctant to write a story for a given title;
- set high standards for themselves and often get frustrated if these are not achieved;
- are able to think analytically;
- enjoy playing with words;
- appreciate humour, ambiguity;
- appreciate different perspectives.

If you study the two lists presented above you will be able to produce a list of children who may be described as *gifted* in English, but the usual words of caution need to be applied here. For all sorts of reasons – fear of teasing, pressure from the teacher, being a second-language learner of English – some children may not show these attributes.

Strategies for effective provision

A useful exercise to undertake, perhaps with a colleague, is to study the list and make a note of the implications for classroom practice. For example, if children enjoy working with words, do they get opportunities to be engaged in some challenging word explorations? Do they look at a fairy-tale and consider different perspectives or create a new version? Do they get opportunities to read widely and talk to the teacher about a masterpiece created by them as part of homework? Do they feel they have to 'wait' to be seen until the others have all finished?

Creating an environment for developing excellence in literacy

In Chapter 3, we discussed ways in which we can create an environment that would be inviting for a child who is linguistically gifted. A language interest centre will have a range of books, word games, word puzzles and squared paper for constructing word searches and crossword puzles. Tape-recorders and tapes should be available. Books, details of their authors and short book reviews would be displayed. Posters illustrating summaries of new books should also add to the interest. Young children should be given opportunities to use dictionaries and a thesaurus. As always, interaction with interested adults plays an important part in developing children's interest in language.

Asking higher order questions

All the adults working with children need to understand what is meant by higher order questions and it is useful to discuss the types of questions one may ask. General principles of questioning were discussed in Chapter 3. In the context of extending language skills, the type of questions which will elicit thoughtful responses are:

- Can you explain why this is so?
- What evidence is there to support this?
- What if the setting was different?
- Do words always sound as they are spelt?
- What letter do you think is used most in the English language?
- Are there similarities between the English language and other languages?

Organising literacy lessons flexibly

As in the case of mathematics lessons, one of the ways in which we can meet the intellectual needs of gifted children is through flexible organisation. For example, children could be provided with opportunities in a range of settings like working in pairs, small groups or participating in whole-class discussions. Some opportunities should also be made available for independent work. Some of the groupings could be on the basis of their ability or interest. For example, you may want to organise pairs to discuss a theme which both children may be interested in, or set a reading task for a group of children who share an interest in a particular author. A small group could be assigned the task for discussion and feedback or for preparing a debate. In these cases children's own particular expertise and skills – in taking notes, summarising, displaying, speaking in a specific style and arguing – could be used.

Independent work can be set for tasks which need extended time, which may be outside the literacy lesson and also be part of homework. Individual children could be set tasks they can share with their peers afterwards. Able language users can often set their own questions effectively and generate text frames. An example of this is given of a young child setting herself the challenge of writing a book in chapters and writing several chapters over a few weeks, and another child undertaking to write to an author (see figures 5.7 and 5.8).

Providing enrichment activities

The examples of activities included in this section should offer intellectually challenging and enjoyable experiences for the gifted young language learner. They should match the needs of such children if you consider the attributes of the children

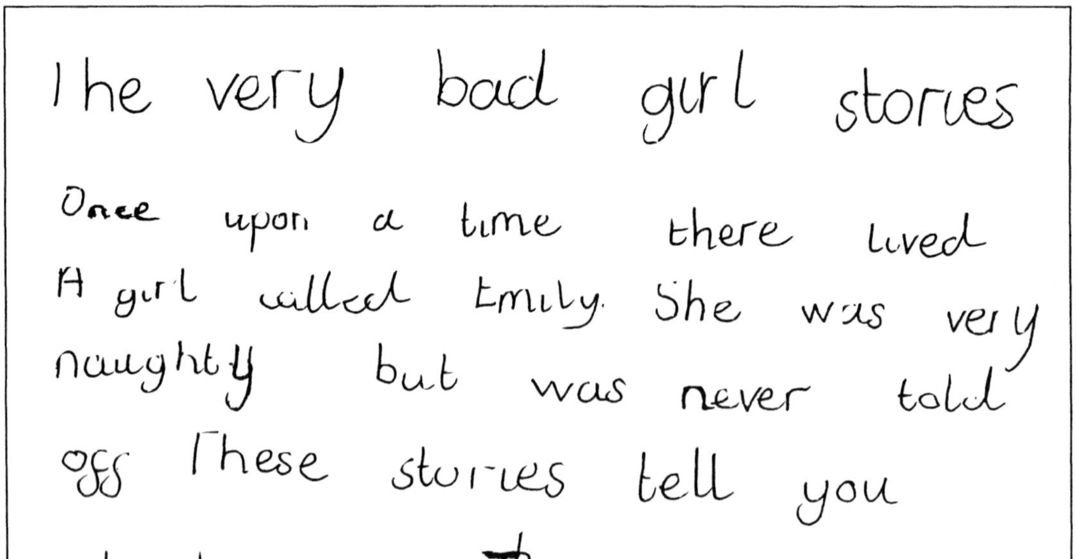

The very bad girl stories

Once upon a time there lived A girl called Emily. She was very naughty but was never told off. These stories tell you about her. The first one is called Painting

Anya
aged 6

Figure 5.7 Writing a book

Hounslow

Cranford Infant School
Berkeley Avenue
Cranford
Hounslow TW4 6LB
telephone 020 8759 0305
fax 020 8754 0208

Meena Walia
Headteacher

Dear Jane Hissy,

I have been reading your story books at school. I have been reading Little bear Lost, Jolly tall, Hoot, Little bears trousers and Jolly Snow. I like all of your books because I like how the characters act. I like of your books but my favirote one is Little bear Lost because Rabbit was not scared to go under the dusty dark bed. I like your pictrues because they are intresting to look at. I forget about reading and look at you pictures and your so good at art. The best pictures you drew was in the book Jolly tall was when they got the big brown box then they tryed opening it. I like funny stories. I like funny stories because they make me laugh. I like other book aswell like this is the bear and the scary night. I am seven years old. I have five friends. I have five people in my family My mum and my dad my sister my brother and me. My birthday is on the 4th of October.

How do you do such good drawings?
What is your favirote thing writing or drawing?
How many books have you wrote?
Are you writing any other new books?

Love
from Jaspreet ♡

Very good Jaspreet. Well done.

I like old bear because he helps all the other toys

Figure 5.8 Letter to an author

as listed in the previous section. The activities suggested below should be suitable for children aged 4 to 7 and may be done at different levels of complexity.

Word explorations

In Chapter 3, I gave examples of an activity inviting children to find words within words. This kind of activity can generate a great deal of interest for all children, especially for the very able. In one 'word within words' lesson the following questions were asked:

- Can you find names of larger animals within the following names of smaller animals? Caterpillar, pigeon...?
- Can you find a smaller animal within the names of these larger animals? Elephant...?

Children have lots of fun working out anagrams, which offers not only a problem-solving activity but a way of learning the correct spellings of words. They may be related to a theme or a current topic. Children may also be asked to invent machines which add suffixes and prefixes to words, and to analyse if they always give clues to the true meaning of the words.

One activity which generated a great deal of interest for a group of seven-year-olds was based on the usefulness of a spell-check on a computer program. Children were asked to attempt the task shown in Figure 5.9.

Tasks which involve analysis, synthesis and evaluation

Some examples of writing tasks which involve higher levels of thinking were presented in earlier chapters. Gifted youngsters demonstrate a higher level of ability in analysing ideas and creating new ones. They also show a greater capability for evaluation. Designing questionnaires for a survey or planning a set of questions to ask a well-known person such as an author, television or sports personality would provide children with opportunities for analysis. Similarly, children's creative imagination can be enhanced by asking them to pretend they are taking the part of a character in a story for a role-play or imagine themselves to be abandoned on a desert island. Examples from a cross-curricular context may be used for this type of work.

The following tasks will enable the gifted language learner to be engaged in higher levels of thinking and in the use of appropriate styles of writing.

- Create a new story after reading one.
- Write a short account of what happened before the opening of the present story.
- Write a sequel to the story.
- Change one of the characters.
- Change the plot.
- Ask: What if this story was written in the present time? What do you think of the way the characters behaved?
- Whose side will you take if you were asked to justify a character's behaviour?

ENGLISH

My computer doesn't understand me

I would like to be a writer when I grow up, but I have a problem, I get the meanings of some words muddled up.

I was given a computer for my birthday, and I know how to use the spell-checker on it. Unfortunately, this does not help. The problem is that my spellings are correct, but it is their meanings that are incorrect. I am told that in the following piece of writing I have done it again, quite a few times. Can you spot where I have gone wrong?

Mark the words which are wrong and replace them with more suitable alternatives.

Long ago, in a far off land, everyone was a frayed. Even the King wore afraid cloak. He had worn the same cloak for years in case the dragon suddenly arrived and he had to run for it. That dragon could Rome anywhere, its fiery breath singeing everything in its path.

"Send for St George," the people cried. "He will sleigh the dragon."

"Send for Father Christmas," shouted others. "Then the dragon can chews a present which will keep him happy."

The local wizard tried killing the dragon with kindness by feeding it dear stew. However, this annoyed the local stags, who complained that by the following spring they would be in a hopeless rut.

Figure 5.9 My computer doesn't understand me

Children need opportunities to use language imaginatively through reading, writing, creating poetry, acting and discussing their ideas. They also need opportunities to share their talents and products with an audience.

Sharing creative products

Finally, work produced in English lessons may be shared with a variety of audiences. This not only helps children to feel that their contributions are valued, but also helps to develop confidence and self-esteem which will lead to greater motivation and fulfilment. Consider the following as opportunities to let children share their products.

- Displays and exhibitions of work to which visitors are invited.
- A presentation in assembly or at parents' evenings.
- Perform ideas in the form of a play or in role-play situations.
- Invite experts to preside over a debate on a topic of current interest.
- Publish regular newsletters giving examples of creative writing, word-puzzles and book reviews.

Developing a flair for English is not just a matter of learning new words, sentence structures, spellings and punctuation. Nuances of meaning, deliberate and unintentional ambiguity and the creation of humorous situations by spotting alternative meanings to those which were intended all add to the enjoyment of learning English, and in my experience, gifted young learners enjoy these opportunities. Those who have linguistic talent should also be given the opportunity to describe imaginary worlds and to create dialogues for animals thought of anthropomorphically – part of a child's skill in creating metaworlds which is arguably an essential ingredient in the reading technique.

Using ICT for enhancing learning opportunities for gifted learners

The aim of this section is to consider how ICT can be used to provide high-quality learning experiences for children. Think for a few moments and write down the range of ICT resources one can have in nursery and infant classrooms. Compare your list with mine which includes a range of resources such as computers, calculators, roamers and floor turtles, tape-recorders, digital cameras, television, video-recorders and all multimedia facilities. Three principles have always guided me when I recommend the use of ICT with young gifted children. First, ICT plays an increasingly important part in our lives and children see that faxes, e-mails, Internet website resources and digital cameras are used in everyday life. Thus it makes sense to start using these with all children. Second, the power and speed offered by many of the resources offer a multitude of opportunities for children who themselves are fast information-processors and quite often have an advanced level of basic knowledge and skills which may then be applied for developing higher level skills such as problem-solving, data-handling, carrying out research, and designing creative activities and presentations. Third, many gifted youngsters I know are capable of working independently and need to be encouraged to do so, and many uses of ICT, especially the computer, can take on the role of a teacher in many contexts. My conviction that ICT offers one of the most effective resources for enhancing educational provision for gifted children is based on observing children using ICT for a number of years. In the following sections, I will draw on some of the experiences I have shared with teachers and children in order to discuss ways in which ICT can be used to extend the learning opportunities for gifted children. However, as always, I maintain that good-quality learning principles for gifted children are always good models of practice for all children.

Before I start presenting examples of ICT at work, I feel it is useful to reflect on some of the attributes of gifted learners which would illuminate why some of the learning experiences and activities I am about to introduce would be suitable. Gifted children, whether their ability is all round or in specific areas:

- learn ideas and techniques quickly;
- ask questions and set their own challenges;
- are capable of independent research;
- are often good readers;
- have higher levels of problem-solving skills;
- are capable of a greater ability to analyse, create and evaluate;
- are capable of crossing subject boundaries when constructing ideas.

With the above in mind in the following sections, I will provide suggestions for practical ways in which we can use ICT with younger children.

Using calculators

During a visit to Singapore three years ago, I was fascinated by the speed and competency shown by young children in using calculators. Having read all the warning lines in the press telling us that calculators are bad for you, I was having doubts whether younger children should use calculators. I need not have worried. Calculators were very much part of the school experiences of children in Singapore and these machines were used only for activities which were designed to extend their problem-solving skills. I was rather pleased when I read a piece in *The Times Education Supplement* (Thompson 1999) where the arguments for using calculators were put forward that Singapore, where the use of calculators was the highest, came top of the list for mathematics performance in the international comparisons. I will include two activities I have used with younger children which should illustrate the level of challenge offered by a calculator as a learning aid. These ideas can be adapted. Readers may be interested to refer to my books – one on numeracy (Koshy 1999) and the other a series of activities for developing mental mathematics (Koshy 2000, listed under Resources) – for further ideas.

Activity 1. Broken keys

You may use only the following keys on your calculator. Can you make up a sum which gives you 100 as the answer?

[3] [4] – + =

Let children work in groups and try different ways. Encourage recording all the trials and the final solution. If you listen to the discussions you will need no further proof of the extent of children's involvement, motivation and mental processing of numbers.

Activity 2. How many minutes have you been alive?

Ask the children to use a calculator to work this out, as the emphasis here is on application and estimation rather than learning or practising multiplication. Again, ask children to record their work so that they can keep a check on where they are going and be able to convince others that the big number they have got is right.

Using roamers and floor turtles

Roamers and floor turtles feature in most primary schools, and young children are often fascinated and excited when they find out that these machines can be made to do things. Floor turtles can be programmed to move 'forward' and 'backward' and turn 'right' or 'left'. They understand units of measure and turns, and by giving sequenced instructions children can make them move and do things. For example, one group of infants dressed up the turtle as a postman and programmed it to deliver letters (Figure 5.10).

Figure 5.10 Floor turtle postman

In another lesson a group of six-year-olds dressed up two roamers and made up a play for them to act by moving around. Think of the challenge involved in programming a roamer to write your name, in Figure 5.11.

Figure 5.11 Roamer challenge

Moving on to screen turtles

It is possible for younger children to work on a programming language referred to as LOGO, where a screen turtle may be programmed to draw shapes and generate number patterns. The latter may be too challenging for many youngsters, but I have seen bright six- and seven-year-olds using LOGO to create shapes and patterns. LOGO originated in the USA where Seymour Papert (1980) described it as 'a simulated micro-world of problem solving for children to explore, discover and form concepts' – all the ingredients we want children to experince. The following examples should illustrate the value of children using LOGO (Figures 5.12 and 5.13).

Collecting presents

Put an acetate sheet on the computer screen and make the turtle get home collecting as many presents as possible on the way. This may be played by a pair or a group of children taking turns.

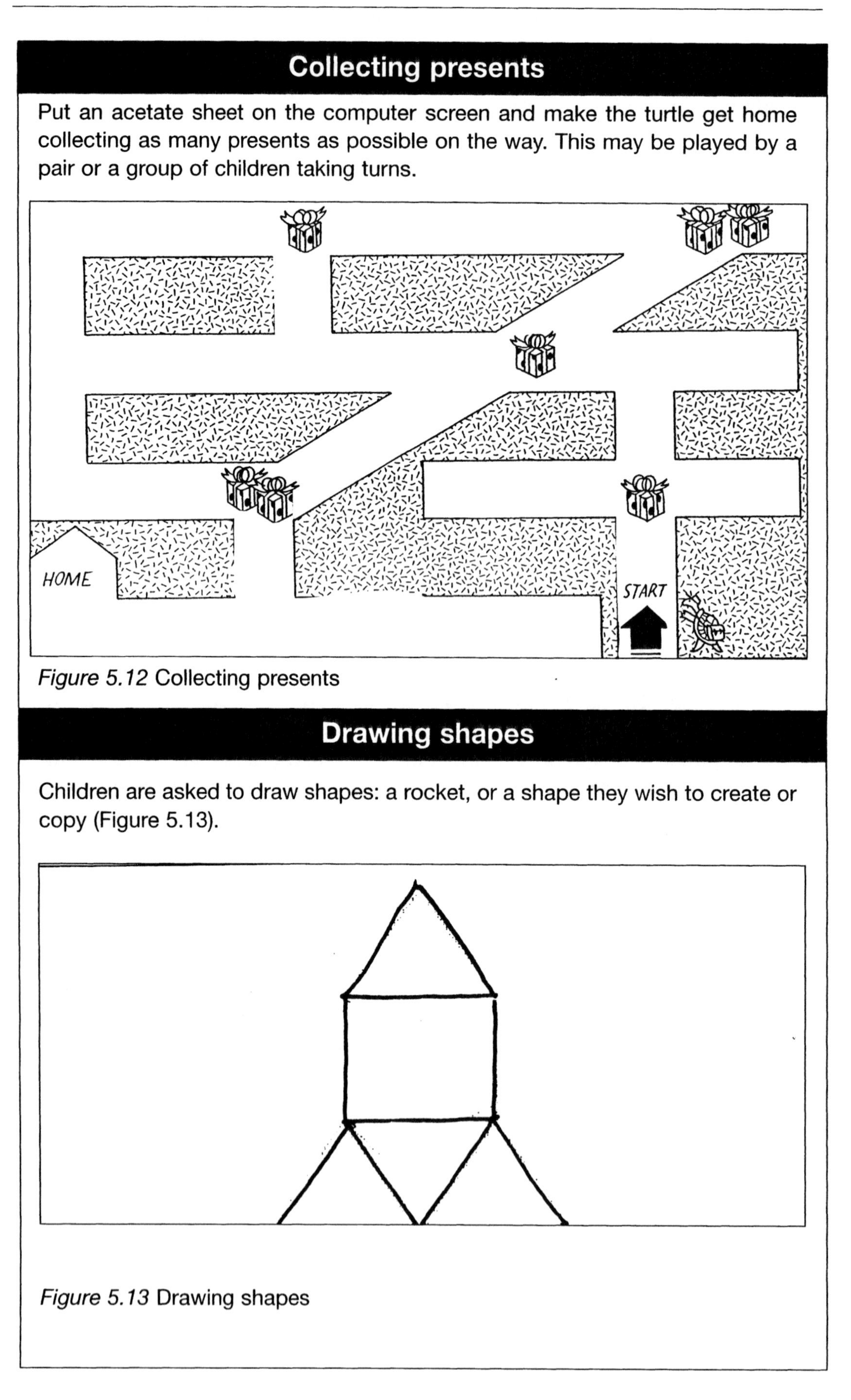

Figure 5.12 Collecting presents

Drawing shapes

Children are asked to draw shapes: a rocket, or a shape they wish to create or copy (Figure 5.13).

Figure 5.13 Drawing shapes

Let us reflect for a moment about what processes are being developed when children work with floor turtles, roamers and screen turtles. They are:

- estimating;
- breaking down a task into manageable parts to solve it;
- planning;
- making mistakes and refining ideas;
- hypothesising;
- finding out that being systematic does help in solving challenging problems.

We often underestimate young children's capacity to use programming languages (HMI 1985).

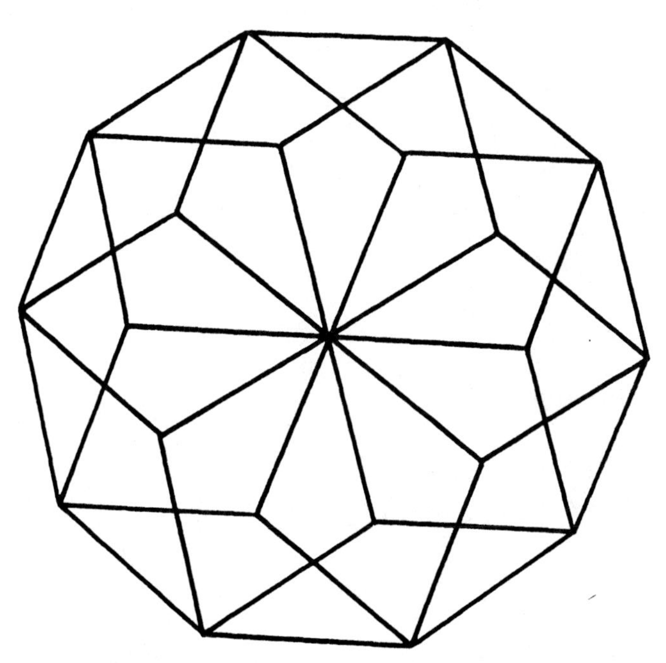

Figure 5.14 LOGO pattern

Figure 5.14 shows an example of what was achieved by infants. Try this with a group of children. Once I observed a group of children taking this on as a challenge and, in preparation for it, their teacher let them use a computer program (SMILE: see Resources) demonstrating the size of angles.

Using databases and spreadsheets

When children use databases, they are engaged in collecting, sorting, analysing, interpreting and representing data. All these processes offer challenges to young children. The following examples will illuminate how using such content-free software can challenge young minds and lead them in conducting enquiries. Besides the training they get for using technology, children enjoy both constructing and interpreting tables and graphs.

Favourite sweets

A Year 1 teacher used a simple database with nursery children to investigate what the class's favourite sweets were. Using a flip-chart she recorded each child's favourite sweet. After the data collection she asked the 'very able' group, with help from a support teacher, to organise input of the data, sorting them out and printing out graphs. A display was set up (Figure 5.15). What was remarkable was that not only the brighter group learned many techniques for creating a database, but the whole class was involved for weeks in discussing the graphs and counting the number of children's choices, and finding out differences and possible reasons for their preferences!

Figure 5.15 Favourite sweets display

Here are some more examples of challenging activities:

- We are setting up a school shop. Can you design a questionnaire (word-processed) to find out what we need to stock it?
- Investigate if there is any truth in the rumour that your height is three times the length of your headband. Your height is the same as your handspan. Boys have bigger heads and so on.

Again, what we see in the above examples are opportunities for children to take the initiative, plan, analyse and disseminate their findings. These activities offer motivating and challenging learning experiences for all children and you may find that the very able children take more responsible roles in such enquiries.

Word-processing

Opportunities for word-processing have made a tremendous impact on enhancing young children's writing and presentation skills. While spelling and handwriting skills need to be developed, access to word-processing can in fact improve the quality and quantity of children's writing. In the case of young, gifted children there may be an added advantage. Children who have very advanced vocabulary and language skills may not always have the physical coordination to write legibly or fluently and may feel frustrated. Using a word-processing package can often help them to produce high-quality work and feel proud of the product. The facilities to draft, edit and save can often help children who are capable of extended writing.

Accessing information

Children who have special interests or who are working on independent projects can access information on the Internet. They can often get expert guidance through websites. Information can be shared with other children who have similar interests through e-mail. There are an increasing number of websites which children can use. The world-class test trial materials and mathematical challenges for the NRICH (see Resources) website are examples of these.

Cross-curricular work

Some of the enrichment activities provided for gifted children would naturally and perhaps ideally cross subject boundaries. The example of a cross-curricular enrichment project in an infant school – Homes for Gnomes – demonstrates how applications of ICT can extend children's thinking. I attended many of the sessions watching children working on this project, and was very impressed with the level of participation and the positive way children responded to the challenges set within this extended project.

The Homes for Gnomes project

The project started with a group of children sitting on the carpet and the teacher, Barbara, reading a fax from Gneville the Senior Gnome (Figure 5.16).

Gnomeland
Gnorwich
Date as postmark

Dear Blue Class,

We have heard about your kindness and great problem-solving abilities and wondered if you could help us.

In Gnomeland it is very cold, too crowded and we don't have enough facilities to support us all. We would like to stay as a community but we need some help to develop a new place to live.

Our requirements are:

- *12 homes, all with 4 rooms of identical size;*
- *we have old retired gnomes and families with children;*
- *each home should have a square garden;*
- *use your imagination to decide what other facilities we need;*
- *we would like a well-planned development.*

Perhaps you could work in groups and send us a number of plans. Also send a letter describing and explaining your decisions.

We trust that you will use your usual kindness and sensitivity to make thoughtful decisions.

Yours gnomely,

Gneville (Senior Gnome)

Figure 5.16 A fax from Gnomeland

Barbara asked the children if they knew what a fax was and responses were invited. She explained what a fax machine did and asked them to look out for one. They brainstormed what they ought to have in the Gnomes estate. Houses, a hospital, a school and perhaps a fish-pond (as '*gnomes like fishing*') were suggested. Before the models of four-cube houses were made, further discussions took place on the type of house they needed to build for the older gnomes, the shape of their gardens, the leisure centre, the need for signposts and so on (Figure 5.17).

Figure 5.17 Planning the Gnomes estate

A plan of the estate and other ideas were sent to the Senior Gnome along with an invitation for the gnomes to come to an exhibition of what might be on offer. Children worked on the following ideas to set up an exhibition (Figure 5.18).

- A logo for Gnomeland
- Names for shops and other buildings
- A gnomes newspaper
- Party invitations
- A poem for the gnomes
- Maps and signposts
- Posters.

Ideas in action shown here bear testimony to the role of ICT for extending children's academic aptitudes, problem-solving skills, creativity, imagination and enterprising spirit. ICT became a facilitator for a challenging project.

Summary

In this chapter I have considered strategies for subject-specific provision. Criteria for subject-specific identification for two subjects – mathematics and English – were presented. A number of strategies for extending the promising mathematician and the able language learner were presented. The role of ICT, with its power and speed, in extending and enriching children's learning was highlighted with practical examples to illustrate how this may be achieved.

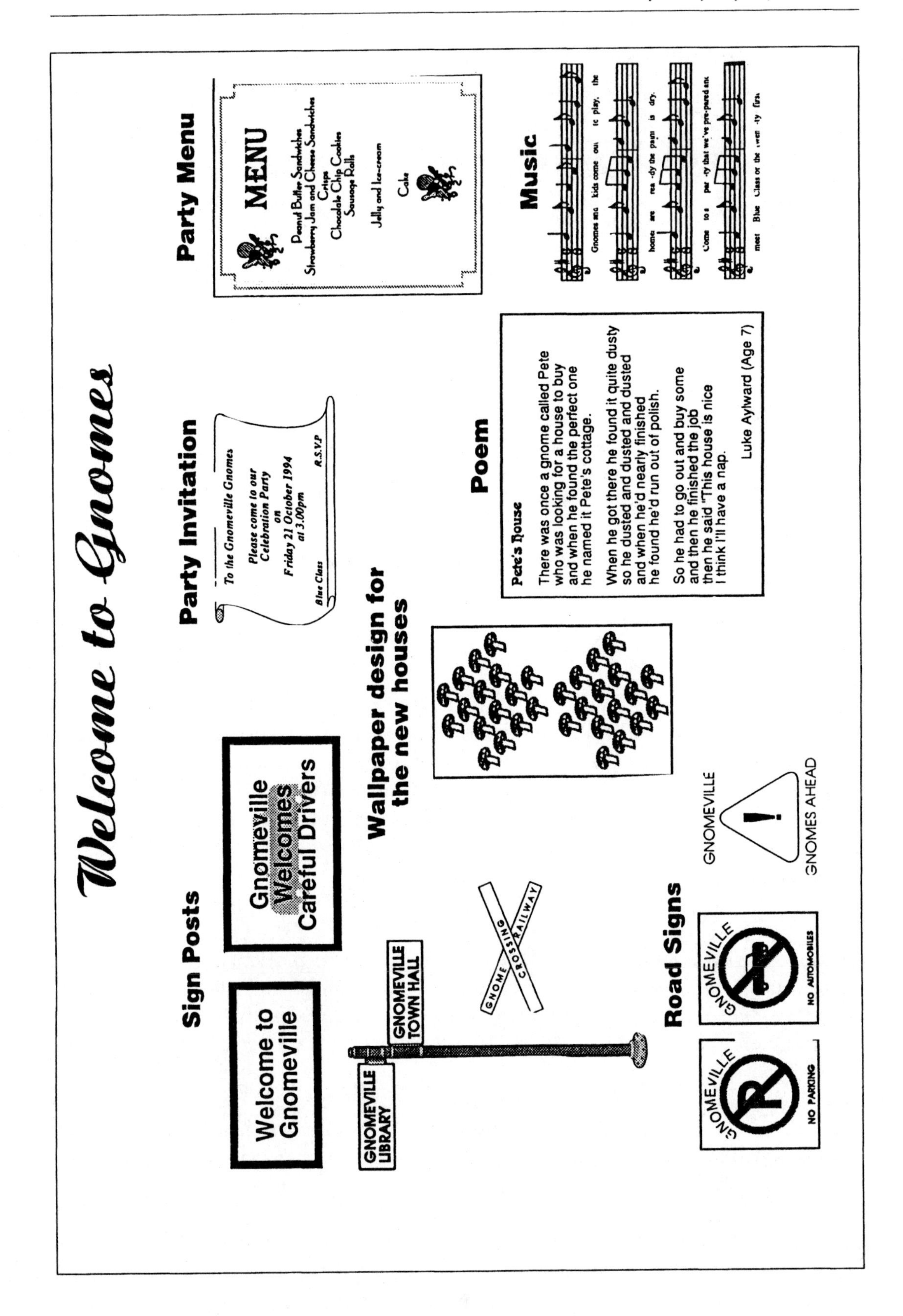

Figure 5.18 Gnomeville: an exhibition

6 Social and emotional needs of younger gifted children

There is much debate on whether gifted children have any particular social and emotional needs. This aspect has not yet received much attention within the national initiatives; nor is there much recent research on the topic in the UK. I have therefore drawn on the case notes kept by my colleagues and myself at the centre for able children on gifted children, and the viewpoints of experts to highlight some relevant issues. I also draw your attention to two authors, Porter (1999) and Stopper (2000) who have addressed the topic of the emotional and social needs of gifted children in two very useful publications. As this book is all about meeting the needs of young, gifted children, I will start this chapter with a quotation cited by Porter from Seligman (1995: 6):

> We want more for our children than healthy bodies. We want our children to have lives filled with friendship and love and high deeds. We want them to be eager to learn and confront challenges ... we want them to grow up with confidence in the future, a love of adventure, a sense of justice, and courage enough to act on that sense of justice. We want them to be resilient in the face of the setbacks and failures that growing up always brings.

These well-articulated aims are desirable goals that we must set for all children, and in this chapter I will explore whether there are some particular challenges with regard to younger gifted children in fulfilling these aims. I use the term 'gifted' to describe children who are cognitively at a much higher level than other children in their age groups. They may have all-round ability and learning potential or marked aptitudes in some specific areas. They are likely to be faster learners and may have a wide range of knowledge which is beyond that of their peer group. They may be capable of thinking at a more sophisticated level and possess higher order skills of problem-solving and analysis. These cognitive attributes can make them feel and act differently which may lead to some special needs and considerations.

When we consider the needs of gifted children it is also important to remember what Baska (1989) reminds us of. She tells us that gifted children appear to be 'out of sync' for their age when we consider normal development expected at any age in the cognitive, emotional and physical realms. She warns us that the mythical 'norm' which has become a bench-mark that schools use, which in any case may fit a very few students, is especially pernicious when applied to the gifted. She maintains the view that although gifted children may excel intellectually, they may be more typical in respect of their physical and emotional development.

Stopper's (2000) view is that it has taken a considerable period for due consideration to be given to the effects of social and emotional development on knowing and thinking and understanding. He maintains that psychological enquiry and brain function research have enabled authors (e.g. Clarke 1988) to develop integrated approaches to education which embrace the premise that thinking, feeling, intuitive and physical sensing functions were interdependent, mutually re-inforcing prerequisites for successful learning and living. Although the main body of literature on gifted education focuses on the cognitive aspects of education, a review of the works by eminent educationists will show that their concept of giftedness does draw attention to aspects of gifted behaviour and definitions of giftedness. For example, Renzulli's 'Three-ring conception of giftedness' (1986), introduced in Chapter 2 includes task commitment, creativity and above-average ability for both the identification and fulfilment of giftedness. The Special Abilities Scales (Koshy and Casey 2000), which was first introduced by Renzulli and Hartman (1971), is an attempt to guide teacher judgement to focus on *behavioural characteristics* and not just the intellectual abilities of children.

The five clusters of characteristics which form the assessment instrument are:

1 Learning characteristics.
2 Social leadership skills.
3 Creative thinking characteristics.
4 Self-determination characteristics.
5 Motivational characteristics.

Significantly, Gardner's (1993) Multiple Intelligences, discussed in detail in Chapter 2, awards interpersonal and intrapersonal intelligences the same status as other intelligences, and the importance of emotional and social aspects in the nurture of giftedness is suggested by Daniel Goleman (1996). A compelling exposition of the interaction between cognitive, emotional, physical and intuitive growth in optimising the development of all individuals is provided by Maslow's (1954) hierarchy of human needs represented by Gomme (2000) in Figure 6.1.

The question is: What can we do within the school situation to enhance the social and emotional needs and well-being of gifted and talented children? Will such enhancement improve their academic achievements?

In Chapter 2, I included a list of both cognitive and affective attributes of gifted children from Silverman (1993). The strategies for effective provision based on these cognitive attributes were discussed in previous chapters. In this chapter, we will look at the affective characteristics of gifted children and consider the implications for action. For the purpose of this discussion, I will use the list of affective characteristics and explanations used by two experts in gifted education, Baska (1989) and Silverman (1993) in the USA. The commentary accompanying them is based on case studies of individual children.

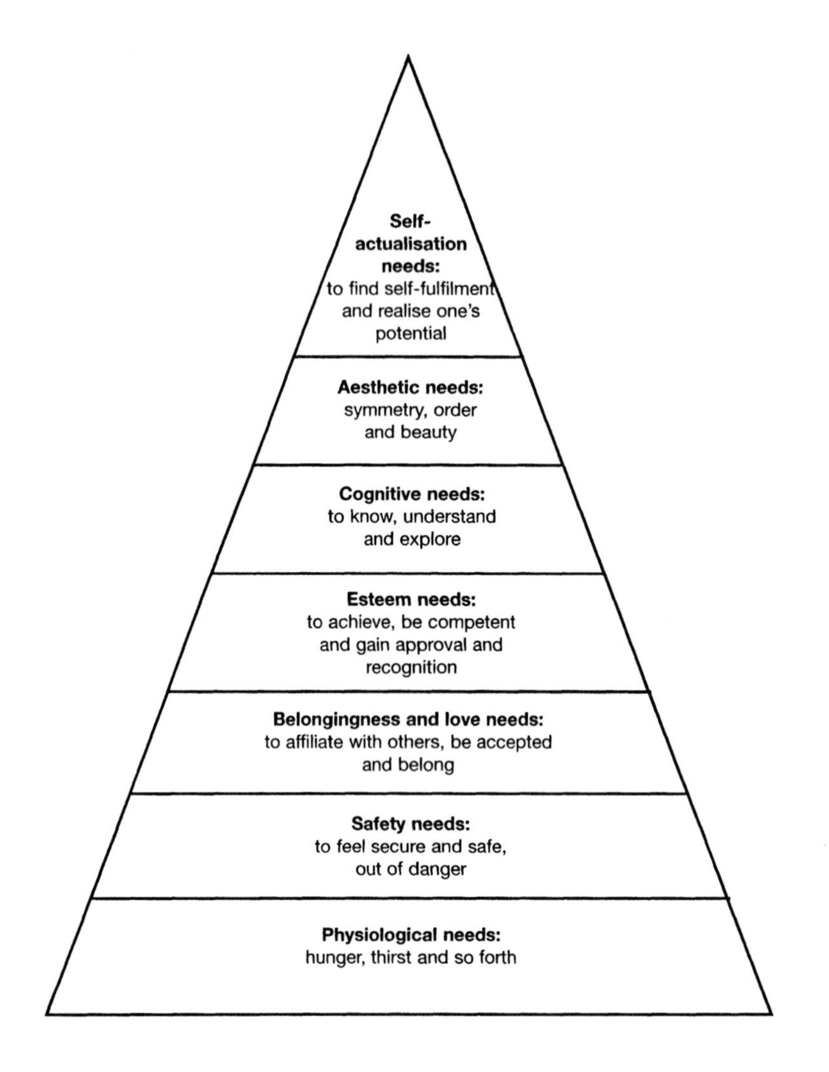

Figure 6.1 Maslow's hierachy of needs

Sense of justice

Baska maintains that gifted children display a strong sense of justice in their human relationships. At later ages they may be attracted to causes that promote social equality. This characteristic reflects general concern for others and also a concern that the world should work in a humane way. This may create tensions in the classroom, as I have seen in one case, when a seven-year-old became very unhappy when he misunderstood the intention of a class project which was in the form of an imaginary competition for winning thousands of pounds. He felt that it was 'very unfair' to win money because 'there are many poor people who have no money at all'.

Emotional intensity

According to Baska, just by being more able cognitively, being able to learn and understand ideas faster, gifted children often experience emotional reactions at a deeper level than do their peers. The ability to emote can make them good at dramatic productions, but this sensitivity may also provoke a negative reaction from other children. These have implications, and the grouping of children of similar ability may help to reduce these reactions. Creating some opportunities for children of higher ability to work together and mix socially may reduce the unpleasant experience of peer group antagonism.

Perfectionism

Baska maintains that many gifted children display perfectionism. They may spend an excessive amount of energy on doing something perfectly and become disturbed if they or others in their environment make mistakes. In our insistence for the 'very best work', we may say and do things which the child may interpret as a desire for perfectionism. I remember one six-year-old tearing up his work several times, and when asked, it was obvious that he felt he was not producing his best. An excessive fear and anxiety which can result from perfectionism may hinder growth or lead a child to develop guilt. This may dissuade a child from engaging in free explorations and prevent growth. Baska reminds us that *'Growth towards excellence, not perfection, is a subtle distinction that teachers and parents must appreciate when working with the gifted child'.*

High levels of energy

Gifted children often show high levels of energy at work and play, Baska tells us. While this energy and fast output may benefit the child in carrying out tasks quickly, it may also be interpreted as being hyperactive. Channelling this energy into meaningful projects and encouragement to persist in responding to challenging activities should help the child to develop self-esteem. A positive use of the high energy is important for the child's emotional development so that boredom, frustration and disruptive behaviour do not develop.

Sense of humour

This is a trait that I have often personally experienced and enjoyed in my work with groups of identified gifted children. They seem to have the ability to appreciate the absurdities and inconsistencies in their surroundings. Their ability to spot patterns and differences may contribute to this trait. Giving them opportunities to share their humour, including their capacity to laugh at themselves, has often made their peers enjoy listening to them and helps make positive relationships.

Divergent thinking ability

Divergent thinkers, according to Lovecky (1993), have a preference for unusual, original and creative responses. The author makes an illuminating observation that divergent thinkers are often high achievers in adulthood, innovative in a number of fields, task-committed, self-starters and independent individuals who use their capacity for innovation and imagination to enhance their emotional well-being. She warns us that in school situations, however, divergent thinkers who ask curious questions, give unusual reponses or dislike working in groups may be viewed negatively. The inevitable non-conformity of these children may lead to frustration, feelings of guilt and lack of acknowledgement and praise from the teachers and other adults. It is important that we are aware of these issues and try to understand the child before dismissing him or her as a day-dreamer or as being difficult to manage. Close observation of children's work, time for an individual interview and consultations with parents should all help to identify such children and offer them support.

Need for mental stimulation

Silverman (1993) highlights the fact that many gifted children crave a great deal of mental stimulation from infancy. Based on infant studies, she points out that precocious infants lose interest in familiar stimuli and prefer novelty. This poses a challenge for the teacher on how to keep the young, gifted child motivated. The two learning traits often cited as attributes of such young children – remarkable memories and an advanced rate of learning – add to the challenge for the teacher. There is certainly a clear need for devising strategies for assessing the child's level of understanding and so provide a matching set of learning experiences. Some of the strategies suggested in previous chapters such as curriculum compacting, independent special projects and ability grouping are worthy of consideration.

In the previous section, I tried to analyse the possible implications, both for our consideration and for offering support to gifted children, in the light of the common attributes associated with gifted children. What I have included is not comprehensive, but is what I feel are the most relevant issues in the context of what I am trying to achieve in this book.

In the absence of support systems and a lack of teacher expertise and knowledge of issues relating to the emotional and social needs of children, the consequence may be underachievement. In the next section I consider possible reasons for underachievement which are directly related to the affective needs of young, gifted children.

Possible reasons for underachievement

Many factors affect the learning process. Lack of motivation and self-esteem, the need for mental stimulation and social acceptance are just some of them. A gifted child may underachieve for the following reasons:

- The child may be aware of his or her potential and may 'switch off' due to the lack of encouragement or opportunities. The 'What is the point?' feeling may set in.
- Ignoring individual learning styles may cause resentment.
- The fear of failure due to perfectionism may tempt the child to hide difficulties and not complete tasks which may be challenging.
- Lack of interest in the topic dealt with may decrease motivation.
- Lack of intellectual stimulation due to a poor match of activities to the ability of the child.
- A gifted child may mask the true level of performance to seek acceptance by peers.
- The nature of the group a child works with may affect motivation. A very able child working in a group where all the other members may be performing at a lower level of cognitive challenge, may find that frustration and resentment set in.

The effects of most of these causes of underacheivement point to children's feelings and emotions. Gaining a clear understanding of the issues is a complex process; we have just made a start.

Making a difference

How can we respond to the emotional and social needs of gifted children? In this section I have tried to provide a list of what I believe may make a difference.

Teacher support

At a recent conference, the participants were asked to list the names of people who have made a significant contribution to their lives. Most of us, perhaps not surprisingly, listed a particular teacher who played a part in making a real difference to our lives. Further discussions revealed that the support given by the teachers were mostly on the affective aspects of our needs; the development of self-esteem as a result of a teacher's praise and encouragement or a special consideration of the difficulties and frustrations experienced by the individual. Understanding the needs of gifted children involves close observation, listening and probing questions. It also requires an understanding of the child's interests, potential strengths and individual learning style.

Exploding the myths

Many adults have misconceptions about gifted children.The most common ones are listed below, along with a short commentary.

- *Gifted children can look after themselves.* It may be true that they can learn new facts and ideas without much help. But they need adults to help them to extend their learning, by providing them with a rich learning environment, and motivating activities and projects for them to pursue.

- *As they know most of what is being taught, they could help other children.* I have often found gifted children to be very willing to be involved in explaining things to others in their peer group, who may be struggling. But an excessive use of this strategy may make a highly able child resentful and would be quite unfair.
- *It is easy to identify gifted children because most of them will identify themselves.* This is only true if the right kinds of opportunities are provided. If the learning programme is motivating and enriching, gifted children will respond and show their strengths. Similarly, if enrichment activities offered are based on their individual aptitude, they are more likely to do their best and show their true potential.

Reducing stress

It does not follow that being gifted always creates stress, but it is likely that some aspects of giftedness may cause some unique situations of stress. Anticipating these can often help the adult to be proactive and support the gifted child. We need to remember that:

- Both over-expectations and lower expectations can affect learning. Over-expectations from parents, teachers or peers can put pressure on the child to a great extent, and as a result the child may decide not to bother. High expectations from adults may be excessive on occasion (Freeman 1995), which can add to children's stress. Lower expectations, on the other hand, leave the child feeling frustrated and can lead to low self-confidence and self-esteem.
- Time constraints and lack of appropriate resources can cause frustration for a creative child, who wishes to pursue a passion or develop a special aptitude in a particular area.
- Gifted children often have a high level of curiosity and may want to ask many questions. But they may feel sensitive to the possible pressure that might be put on their teacher's time.
- Gifted children feel pressurised to live up to the label of being very bright and feel reluctant to ask for help even when it is needed.
- A child who is reflective and happy to work alone may feel inadequate because of the feeling that socialising and working in groups are the norm.

The school context

The final section of this chapter is devoted to ways in which a gifted child's emotional and social development may be enhanced within the school context.

Celebrating success

Children are often full of admiration for peers who show exceptional talent in music, sports, drama or art. Many of the problems reported to me in the context of gifted children arise from the resentment felt by other children towards children who are academically very gifted. Teasing and bullying very bright children are common in all sorts of schools. One of the ways in which this can be tackled is to rethink the school ethos and consider if adults who work with children celebrate success in all areas equally. It may be necessary to make a deliberate attempt to highlight that all achievements are given equal status.

Encourage peer relations

A few years ago, when I first met a group of nominated gifted youngsters, as an ice-breaker activity I suggested that all of us say a few words about how our friends would describe us. Within a few minutes, I realised this was not a wise strategy to use at the start of a workshop, because some of them told me that they did not have any friends. One young boy, Steven, told me, *'Clever children don't have many friends'*. How can we help? While we want to encourage socialisation in school, some of the traits and interests of gifted children may make it difficult for them to make friends with others in their peer group. In the context of the above-mentioned workshop, I realised why some of them would find it difficult to form peer-group friendships. Often, their interests were quite different from those of other children; for example, one five-year-old spent her spare time making up games with very complex rules. The other children in the group could relate to these rules and were full of admiration for her. Another child was interested in the *greenhouse effect* and wondered how we could do something about it. In a school situation, these types of interest are unlikely to appeal to other children of their age. This can pose a problem. As it is unlikely that there would be many children within a school with such unique interests, we need to think about specific strategies to help these children. During a visit to the USA, my hostess took me to a centre where exceptionally able younger children met twice a week to pursue their particular interests. I was curious to find out what the thinking behind having a special centre was, and asked her. I was told, *'Well, if we have them working within the normal classroom they will be frustrated and lose their confidence and self-esteem. They will start thinking that they have strange and weird interests, but if we keep them here at the centre all the time, they will only meet other children who are very similar to them. In real life this could do them some harm.'*

Having interest groups, or arranging the support of an *understanding* and *enthusiastic* mentor or enabling them to attend outside school clubs may help these children to accept their unique and exceptional abilities as a positive feature. Making use of the community for volunteer mentors and encouraging parents to enrol their children in clubs where they can work and socialise with children who may have similar levels of ability are also helpful ways forward.

The aim of schooling is to help to develop the 'whole' child by meeting both his or her cognitive and affective needs. Gifted young children do have special needs and therefore we have responsibilities to meet those needs. A fitting conclusion to this chapter is given by Silverman (1993: 3), in referring to gifted children:

> We have a moral responsibility to do more than fill their minds with knowledge. Knowledge without wisdom and ethics is dangerous. We cannot inculate the values we desire, but we can inspire their development through our own attitudes

and actions. We are these children's role models, and we embody these in our own lives, we teach them more from who we are than anything we say or do. And we will learn from them as well.

Summary

In this chapter we considered ways in which we can meet the affective needs of gifted children. As is reflected in recent lierature on the identification of giftedness, there is an increasing awareness that feelings, temperaments, attitudes, task commitment and other behavioural aspects can infuence the fulfilment of children's potential. An attempt has been made to analyse the characteristics attributed to gifted children to consider their particular needs so that we can devise strategies to help them. How children's lack of self-esteem, cognitive stimulation and social acceptance may affect their learning was considered. The final section of the chapter was devoted to a consideration of how schools can respond to the emotional and social needs of gifted children.

7 Selecting and using resources for gifted children

Before discussing aspects of selecting and using resources for teaching gifted young children, let us reflect on what we are aiming for. Based on the principle of the two-way process of provision and identification, the following may be summarised as our aims:

- Providing children with an intellectually challenging teaching programme to extend their knowledge and conceptual understanding.
- Allowing children sufficient freedom for exploration and using their imagination.
- Acknowledging children's creativity and individual learning styles.
- Identifying children's strengths and talents – both in general and domain-specific terms – and using that knowledge as a basis for provision.
- Being aware of the particular social and emotional needs gifted children may have.
- Recognising the important role played by adults both for identification and provision.

Although many of the points raised above have been discussed in previous chapters, it is important to reiterate these principles here. It is also important to remind ourselves that resources are a means to an end and, in the context of this book, the resources we select should enable us to achieve excellence in provision for young, gifted children.

Selection and choice of resources

The teacher

The most valuable resource for educating gifted children within the school situation is the teacher. I therefore feel it is important that we start with a consideration of the attributes of an effective teacher of young gifted children. Before reading on, you might want to make a list of what those attributes may be. What I have included in the following list has emerged from my discussion with teachers on in-service courses focusing on provision for young gifted children. So, what are those characteristics?

The attributes of a teacher of the young, gifted child

Consider the following features. Are they desirable attributes in a teacher who is committed to making the best provision for able pupils? One could, of course, rightly argue that these attributes are desirable for all teachers.

FLEXIBILITY

Teachers of gifted children need to be flexible in several respects. They need to be flexible in their identification process. They need to employ a range of methods of identification, using multiple sources of information, described in Chapter 2. They need to be aware of the individual learning styles of the children and be prepared to let children work in flexible ways – in groups or individually. Classroom materials should be used flexibly and curriculum content needs to be designed in such a way that it matches the needs of the child as closely as possible. Teachers should be open-minded and flexible enough to accept that some curriculum compacting may be necessary to avoid frustration and boredom for the child.

INTEREST IN APPROPRIATE PROFESSIONAL DEVELOPMENT

Teachers of young, gifted children often show enthusiasm for finding out all aspects of gifted education. In my experience, thay have always been very enthusiastic about their own professional development in aspects of giftedness. They appreciate opportunities for considering appropriate ways of identifying children's strengths. They realise that with some support much of what they are already doing could be modified, refined and refocused to make it appropriate for the needs of the gifted child. Attendance at an in-service course to update their own knowledge and current thinking would be an integral part of teachers' development. In a survey carried out by our centre, teachers listed the following as the most useful aspects of the in-service course they attended.

- Questioning skills.
- Curriculum differentiation strategies.
- Identification of specific intelligences (Gardner 1993).
- Setting up of interest centres and carrying out semi-structured observations.
- Emotional and social needs of young gifted children.

EXCELLENCE MUST BECOME A HABIT

As I have emphasised in all my writings, the teacher needs to set high expectations and recognise that excellence in teaching and learning should become a habit. This involves providing high-quality activities and resources. Organising displays of pupils' best work will help to communicate the idea that the school sets very high standards. Gifted children will have much to contribute to these displays. Textbooks and bought lesson plans would be used very selectively, if at all. Children's special interests and hobbies would be acknowledged. A rich classroom environment will be provided.

LEARNING IN PARTNERSHIP

The teacher would send the message that no one knows about everything but can always find out more through research. Children would be reassured that making mistakes is acceptable, and leads to the joyous experience of making discoveries and producing pleasing products. It is a good idea to reinforce the fact that many famous people have worked for long periods of time to achieve something of significance. Teachers would also be aware of the particular social and emotional needs of gifted children and address these proactively. Having a sense of humour and being able to create a relaxed atmosphere will certainly help. The teacher needs the confidence of a creative gardener capable of the excitement of a special rose in bloom combined with the humility to recognise that its beauty has been hers to nurture, though it was not of her creation.

MENTORS AS FACILITATORS FOR GIFTED CHILDREN

The use of a mentor to support the gifted child was mentioned previously. Carefully selected mentors provide an invaluable resource for the development of the gifted child. A study of many famous people who have made significant achievements in life has highlighted the important role played by a mentor who facilitated their development by providing guidance. The mentor may be relative. Einstein is said to have developed his interest in mathematics through playing mathematical games with an uncle. It is often claimed that having a mentor can make a significant impact on the attitudes and achievements of a gifted child. A mentor is someone who can provide guidance for the gifted child to develop. The mentor would ideally have the respect and admiration of the child. A mentor may come from the community or from a local higher education institution or a secondary school. The mentor can often provide a useful role model for the child and have knowledge in the field of the child's interest. I have known two children whose attitudes to learning and behaviour were considerably enhanced when the school arranged mentors for them. Six-year-old John, whose case study was presented in Chapter 1, demonstrated a marked aptitude for mathematics, and the school found it difficult to meet his mathematical development within the classroom. Due to his small size and poor physical coordination he was not moved up to an older class for his mathematics lessons. Instead, the school obtained the help of a mathematics specialist from the local secondary school who visited John at his own school. The mentor spent two one-hour sessions with John every week, discussing mathematics and the achievements of well-known mathematicians. In the second example, a seven-year-old child who was very advanced in all subjects and was the target of much teasing and even bullying was introduced to a mentor from a sixth-form college who visited him once a week and discussed his work and interests. In this instance, much of the mentoring was counselling the child by listening to him and supporting him. According to the child's teacher, the presence of a mentor changed his life, and he 'blossomed into a confident little boy', as she put it. These two success stories did not happen by accident. In both cases the school selected the mentors carefully and the results were pleasing.

The following features may be present in a mentor. He or she

- would be older than the child;
- would have a strong interest and possible expertise in the field of the child's interest;
- would be flexible and help the child to evaluate, reflect and refine ideas;
- would help the child to set realistic goals and plan rewarding experiences;
- would show understanding and empathy.

A SCHOOL AUDIT

Does your school meet the needs of young gifted children? Here is a possible checklist which you could use for an audit.

- Does the school have a set of policy guidelines covering the needs of gifted children?
- Do all members of staff know the contents of the policy?
- Do you draw information from multiple sources for identifying gifted and talented children?
- What steps are taken to consider underachievement of pupils with high potential?
- Does the school enlist the partnership of parents for identifying talent and in making effective provision?
- Does the school have support from any external agencies?
- What is done to celebrate exceptional achievement?
- Has any staff development taken place in recent years?
- Is a list of resources made available to all staff?
- Do displays reflect high expectations using high-quality products?

Based on the audit, action needs to be taken. If necessary, a policy needs to be compiled and disseminated. The policy needs to be concise, succinct and clear. Possible headings for the policy may include: Rationale; Aims; Views of ability; Identification methods; Provision: framework for curriculum differentiation, interest centres, quality of questions and so on; Learning and teaching styles; External support; Resources.

Resources

A range of readings and resources have been referred to in the text and are listed in the Reference section. In addition to these, the following sources offer support for gifted pupils either in the form of materials or as guidance.

Recommended reading

Gardner, H. (1983) *Frames of Mind.* New York: Basic Books. *This book provides a framework for understanding the Multiple Intelligences concept of identification.*

Koshy, V. and Casey, R. (1997) *Special Abilities Scales.* London: Hodder & Stoughton. *This handbook gives a summary of behavioural characteristics for identification.*

Teaching resources

1 Casey, R. and Koshy, V. (1995) *Bright Challenge*, 7–11 years.
2 Koshy, V. (ed) (1997) *Infant Challenges*, 4–7 years.
The first book contains activities for able pupils in mathematics, English and science. The second provides challenging starting points for children aged 4–7. *Details of both books may be obtained from Valsa Koshy, The Brunel Able Children's Education Centre (address is listed later in this chapter).*

Mathematics resources

The following excellent resources are available from The Association of Teachers of Mathematics (ATM) Publications, 7 Shaftesbury Street, Derby DE23 8YB (Tel. 01332-346-599).

- *Exploring Mathematics with Younger Children.*
- *Points of Departure Books 1 and 2.*
- *Teaching, Learning and Mathematics with IT.*

Write to: Tarquin Publications, Stradbroke, Diss, Norfolk IP21 5JP (Tel. 01379-384-218) for a catalogue. Excellent materials are available in this catalogue.
Koshy, V. (2000) *Mental Mathematics*, ages 5–7, 7–9 and 9–11. London: Collins.

Computer-based resources

British Educational Communications and Technology Agency (BECTA – used to be known as NCET) (*http://www.ncet.org.uk*) provides a useful list of support systems for using ICT.

BECTA, Millburn Hill Road, Science Park, Coventry CV4 7JJ.

SMILE provides a good range of software to support mathematics teaching. The programs are differentiated at levels of challenge and provide feedback.

SMILE, Isaac Newton Centre, 108a Lancaster Road, London W11 1QS.

Websites

The National Association of Teachers in English (*http://www.nate.org.uk*)
NRICH (*http://nrich.maths.org.uk/*): an online maths club which should be of particular help for extension activities.
Maths ideas (*http://www.teachingideas.co.uk/maths/contents.htm*)
AIMS puzzle page (*http://www.aimsedu.org/Puzzle/PuzzleList.html*)
Site with challenging problems and information (*http://www.cut-the-knot.com/*)
World-class tests for gifted children, QCA (*http://www.qca.org.uk*)

Teacher support materials

QCA (2001) *Working with Gifted and Talented Children (Key Stages 1 and 2)*: an in-service pack, video and exemplar materials.

A series of books: *Stories for Thinking, Games for Thinking, Poems for Thinking*. Oxford: Nash Pollock.

DfES (2000) *National Literacy and Numeracy Strategies: Guidance on Teaching Able Children*. London: DfES.

Support organisations

1 **The Brunel Able Children's Education centre (BACE)**, School of Education,

Brunel University, 300 St Margaret's Road, Twickenham TW1 1PT.
Writes curriculum materials, researches into aspects of gifted education and provides training programmes on the 'gifted' for teachers of all key stages. Short courses and conferences are offered for coordinators and others.

2 **Children of High Intelligence**, PO Box 4222, London SE22 8XG.

Runs Saturday classes and provides support for children and parents.

3 **Gift**, The International Study Centre, Dartford Grammar School, West Hill, Dartford, Kent DA1 2HW.

Provides enrichment programmes for pupils, teacher support courses and materials.

4 **National Association for Able Children in Education (NACE)**, Westminster College, Oxford OX2 9AT.

Provides teacher support and a range of materials. NACE also provides short courses and conferences.

5 **National Association for Gifted Children (NAGC)**, Elder House, Milton Keynes MK9 1LR.

Provides support for parents. NAGC offers Saturday clubs and produces materials for teachers.

Summary

In this chapter I discussed aspects of selecting resources for gifted children. The attributes of an effective teacher of the gifted were highlighted. A brief checklist was provided to facilitate an audit of provision in a school along with some useful headings for compiling a policy statement. The rest of the chapter was devoted to listing useful resources: books, packs of ideas, ICT based support and some useful websites.

References

Alexander, R., Rose, J. and Woodhead, C. (1992) *Curriculum Organisation and Classroom Practice in Primary Schools*. London: DES.
Association of Teachers in Mathematics (ATM) (1993) *Exploring Mathematics with Younger Children*. Derby: ATM.
Baska, L. K. (1989) 'Characteristics and needs of the gifted' in Feldhusan, J., Van Tassel-Baska, J. and Seeley, K. (eds) *Excellence in Educating the Gifted*. Colorado: Love Publishing.
Beecher, M. (1996) *Developing the Gifts & Talents of All Students*. Connecticut: Creative Learning Press.
Black, P. and William, D. (1998) 'Assessment and classroom learning', *Assessment in Education*, **5** (1).
Bloom, B. S. (1956) *Taxonomy of Educational Objectives*, Volume 1. London: Longman.
Carbo, M., Dunn, R. and Dunn, K. (1991) *Teaching Students to Read Through Their Individual Learning Styles*. Boston, MA: Allyn & Bacon.
Casey, R. and Koshy, V. (2001) *Bright Challenge* Key Stage 2. (*see* Resources).
Clarke, B. (1988) *Growing up Gifted*. Columbus: Charles. E. Merril.
Daily Telegraph (1996) 'A brighter start to the weekend', 16th October.
David, T. (ed.) (1999) *Teaching Young Children*. London: Paul Chapman.
DfEE (1997) *Excellence in Schools*. London: Department for Education and Employment.
DfEE (1998) *DfEE News*, April. From Estelle Morris, Education Minister. London: DfEE.
DfEE (1999) *Excellence in Cities*. London: Department for Education and Employment.
DfES (2000a) *National Literacy and Numeracy Strategies: Guidance on Teaching Able Children*. London: Department for Education and Skills.
DfES (2000b) *Mathematical Challenges for Able Pupils in Key Stages 1 and 2*. London: Department for Education and Skills.
Eyre, D. (2001) 'An effective primary school for the gifted', in Eyre, D. and Mc Clure, L. (eds) *Curriculum Provision for the Gifted and Talented*. London: David Fulton Publishers.
Freeman, J. (1995) 'Annotation: recent studies of giftedness in children', *Journal of Child Psychology and Psychiatry*, **36**(4), 531–47.
Freeman, J. (1998) *Educating the Very Able. Current International Research*. London: Ofsted.
Gardner, H. (1983) *Frames of Mind*. New York: Basic Books.
Gardner, H.(1993) *Multiple Intelligences*. New York: Basic Books.
Gardner, H. (1999) *Intelligence Reframed. Multiple Intelligences for the 20th Century*. New York: Basic Books.
Goleman, D. (1996) *Emotional Intelligence*. London: Bloomsbury.
Gomme, S. (2000) 'The role of the family', in Stopper, M. (ed.) *Meeting the Social and Emotional Needs of Gifted and Talented Children*. London: NACE/David Fulton Publishers.
HMI (1985) *Mathematics 5–16: Curriculum Matters 3*. London: HMSO.
HMI (1992) *Education Observed: The Education of Very Able Pupils in Maintained Schools*. London: HMSO.
House of Commons (1999) Education and Employment Select Committee. Third Report. *Highly Able Children*. London: HMSO.
Howe, M. (1998) *Principles of Abilities and Human Learning*. Hove, East Sussex: Psychology Press.
Koshy, V. (1999) *Effective Teaching of Numeracy for the National Mathematics Framework*. London: Hodder & Stoughton.
Koshy, V. (2001) *Teaching Mathematics to Able Children*. London: David Fulton Publishers.
Koshy, V. and Casey, R. (1997a) 'Empowering the teacher to meet the challenge of the able child', *Early Childhood and Care*, **130**, 49–58.

Koshy, V. and Casey, R. (1997b) *Effective Provision for Able and Exceptionally Able Children*. London: Hodder & Stoughton.

Koshy, V. and Casey, R. (2000) *Special Abilities Scales*. London: Hodder & Stoughton.

Krutetskii, V. A. (1976) *The Psychology of Mathematical Abilities in School Children*. Chicago, Il: University of Chicago Press.

Lovecky, D. (1993) 'The quest for meaning: counselling issues with gifted children and adolescents', in Silverman, L. (ed.) *Counselling the Gifted and Talented*. Colorado: Love Publishing.

Marland Report (1972) US Education Department.

Maslow, A. (1954) *Motivation and Personality*. New York: Harper & Row.

Mitchell, C. and Koshy, V. (1995) *Effective Teacher Assessment: Looking at Children's Learning*. London: Hodder & Stoughton.

Morelock, M. and Morrison, K. (1996) *Gifted Children Have Talents Too*. Australia: Hawker Brownlow Education.

Office for Standards in Education (Ofsted) (1993) *First Class*. London: Ofsted.

Office for Standards in Education (Ofsted) (1994) *Exceptionally Able Children*. Report of conferences. London: Ofsted.

Office for Standards in Education (Ofsted) (2001) *Providing for Gifted and Talented Pupils: An Evaluation of Excellence in Cities and other grant-funded programmes*. London: Ofsted.

Ogilvie, E. (1973) *Gifted Children in Primary Schools*. London: Macmillan.

Papert, S. (1980) *Mindstorms: Children, Computers and Powerful Ideas*. New York: Basic Books.

Parnes, S. J. (1982) 'Education and Creativity', in Vernon. P. E. (ed.) *Creativity*. London: Penguin.

Porter, L. (1999) *Gifted Young Children*. Buckingham: Open University Press.

QCA (1999) *Early Learning Goals*. London: QCA Publications.

Renzulli, J. (1986) 'The three-ring conception of giftedness: a developmental model for creative productivity', in Sternberg, R. J. and Davidson J. E. (eds) *Conceptions of Giftedness*. Cambridge: Cambridge University Press.

Renzulli, J. (1994) *Schools for Talent Development: A Practical Plan for School Improvement*. Connecticut: Creative Learning Press.

Renzulli, J. and Hartman, R. (1971) 'Scale for rating behavioural characteristics of superior students', *Exceptional Children*, **38**(3) 243–8.

Rutter, M. and Rutter, M. (1992) *Developing Minds. Challenges and Continuity Across the Life Span*. New York: Basic Books.

Seligman, M. E. P. (1995) *The Optimistic Child*. Sydney: Random House.

Sheffield, L. (1994) *The Development of Gifted and Talented Mathematics Students and the National Council of Teachers of Mathematics Standards*. Connecticut: The National Research Centre on the Gifted and Talented.

Silverman, L. (1993) *Counselling the Gifted and Talented*. Colorado: Love Publishing.

Sternberg, R. (1986) 'A triarchic theory of intellectual giftedness', in Sternberg R. J. and Davidson J. E. (eds) *Conceptions of Giftedness*. Cambridge: Cambridge University Press.

Stopper, M. (ed.) (2000) *Meeting the Social and Emotional Needs of Gifted and Talented Children*. London: NACE/David Fulton Publishers.

Straker, A. (1982) *Mathematics for Gifted Pupils*. London: Longman.

Sylva, K. (1994) 'School influences of children's development'. *Journal of Child Psychology and Psychiatry and Related Disciplines*, **35**(1) 135–70.

Sylva, K. (1998) *Too Much Too Soon?* Keynote address given at the Islington Early Years conference, 9 July.

Thomas, L., Casey, R. and Koshy, V. (1996) *Teachers' Perceptions on Provision for Able Children in England and Wales*. Paper presented at the AERA Conference, New York.

Thompson, I. (1999) 'Prop or Tool', *The Times Education Supplement*, 12 March.

Van Tassel-Baska, J. (1992) *Planning Effective Curriculum for Gifted Learners*. Denver, CO: Love Publishing.

Vygotsky, L. (1978) *Mind in Society*. Cambridge: Harvard University Press.

Index

Printed in the United Kingdom
by Lightning Source UK Ltd.
109923UKS00002B/141-154